BRIGHT EMINENCE

*   *   *

The Life and Thought of
JACOB RADER MARCUS
Scholar, Mentor, Counsellor,
for Three Generations of Rabbis and
Lay Leaders of American Jewry

BRIGHT EMINENCE

✳✳✳✳✳✳✳✳✳✳✳✳✳✳✳✳✳✳✳✳✳

The Life and Thought of
JACOB RADER MARCUS:
Scholar, Mentor, Counsellor,
for Three Generations of Rabbis and
Lay Leaders of American Jewry

By RANDALL M. FALK

Introduction by DR. ALFRED GOTTSCHALK

Joseph Simon *Pangloss Press*

MALIBU, CALIFORNIA

Library of Congress Cataloging-in-Publication Data

Falk, Randall M.
    Bright eminence : memoirs of Jacob Rader Marcus : scholar, mentor,
counsellor for three generations of rabbis and lay leaders of American Jewry /
by Randall M. Falk ; with an introduction by Alfred Gottschalk.
       p.   cm.
    ISBN 0-934710-29-5
    1. Marcus, Jacob Rader, 1896-   . 2. Rabbis—United States—Biog-
raphy. 3. Jewish historians—United States—Biography. I. Title.
BM755.M327F35   1994
973'.04924024—dc20   93-44498
   [B]   CIP

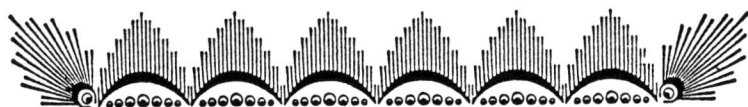

CONTENTS

5

For my children
Randall Marc, Jonathan and
Debra, Christopher and Heidi
privileged to be among the many
adopted nieces and nephews
of their beloved "Dr. Jake"

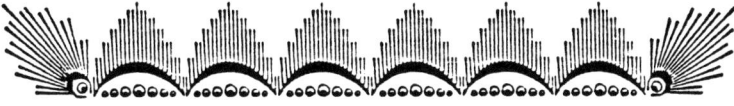

JACOB R. MARCUS: A TRIBUTE

THIS VOLUME, which is dedicated to Jacob R. Marcus, is a testament to the life of the mind. Professor Marcus is the academic man, *par excellence*. He is devoted to the most rigorous and thorough scholarship, unfiltered through personal predilections or pet theories. Although he has generalized about what he has understood to be the matrix of history, especially Jewish history, he does not enter his research with a mindset to evolve particular solutions to questions of historiography which are the underpinnings of all speculation about the meaning of the events of the past.

Marcus, unlike other historians, but very much like Heinrich Graetz, sees the unfolding of Jewish history, not as a series of lachrymose historic cycles, relieved now and then by epochs of hope and the budding of Jewish genius, but as an unfolding of the spirit of an eternal people within the context of time. Heinrich Graetz, in his work, "The Construction of Jewish History," which was the ground plan for his multi-volume classic of "The History of the Jews," served in every respect as a model for Marcus.

Marcus evolved a methodology comparable to that of Graetz, for dealing with the unchartered sea of history. As an avid student of medieval times, he chartered the evolution of communal sick care, as well as the social infrastructure that was the environment of Jews living in medieval times. Marcus taught us how to use community records, minute books, all sorts of written evidence, letters, memoirs, and community ledgers, in piecing together the vast jigsaw puzzle of Jewish life in the Middle Ages. He also had a great fascination with the status of the Jew in Germany. His fascination with Jews living in an emancipated environment, yet subject to a major decline and ultimately a holocaust, left an indelible imprint upon his person and inherent optimism. When it was clear that the chapter of German Jewish history had come to an end at Auschwitz, Marcus turned his eyes to the American Jewish experience. There he discovered the emergence of the greatest Jewry the Diaspora has ever known. Marcus pioneered the study of American Jewish history. It seems somewhat incongruous that Jews who have lived in America over 200 years had no historian to chart their course on the new continent in the *goldene medinah*. Marcus wrote extensively on the utilization of historical materials for the structuring of American Jewish historical research.

Marcus pioneered the original methodological framework, upon which others have built their own patterns of the evolution of the American Jewish experience. Facts are always of primary concern for Marcus. They are the bricks out of which the structure of history is built. They are, one by one and in the aggregate, the foremost reliable elements in our understanding of the past. How the facts fit together to build a structure comprehensible and understandable as a pattern of Jewish history gives Marcus pause for thought.

As an eminent historian, Marcus has observed that, "Books are the memory of mankind. A people that is not conscious of its past has no assurance of a future." Throughout the many years of his precious life, Marcus has never taken his gifts of mind and heart for granted. He has worked very hard at what he does and, consequently, his work will stand the test of time. To the best of his ability, he has produced an oeuvre that is his legacy to the Jewish people in America and to other historians who study and seek to understand American Jewish life.

There was much debate in 19th-century England as to whether great men shape history or whether history shapes great men. Thomas Carlyle, in his work on "Heroes and Hero Worship," tends to the notion that history is, indeed, shaped by great personages. Marcus partakes of that view to a great extent, and, therefore, he is interested in the biographies and the contributions that individuals have made to America and to Jewish life. He is cognizant of the fact that the tide of events often sweeps us along, and it is the rare hero that steps forward to attempt to swim upstream against the tide and rise above it to assert both will and principle. Marcus is an admirer of the true hero who contributes to civilization, and who helps to shape the world of tomorrow.

There is much in Marcus' makeup that presents a man who, in some ways, is an enigma. For one who is passionately attached to the world of facts, he is also attached passionately to his colleagues and friends, to other people who care for him and about whom he cares. He has nurtured a generation of young historians through his personal supervision of their work. He has assisted neophyte scholars and guided them through a very careful but constructive criticism of their research. He has also been, for many of us, a rabbi, a counsellor, a confidant, and for those who are most fortunate, to have him as a friend. He gives of himself without stint and, truly, at his august age, gives of his time to those who are in need of his wisdom.

This volume, which presents his life and work, will speak for itself. As Marcus himself has often observed, we are living in a time in which we are experiencing a "golden age" in American Jewish life and, indeed, in world Jewish history. Marcus' writing and lecturing in his inimitable manner, helped illuminate that epoch for us who are privileged to call him their mentor and friend. We truly wish for him the continuation of his long and fruitful life. May God con-

9

tinue to bless the work of his hands and establish his work as the legacy to future generations.

DR. ALFRED GOTTSCHALK
President
Hebrew Union College/Jewish
Institute of Religion

FOREWORD

Ⅰ N HIS NINETY-EIGHTH YEAR, Jacob Rader Marcus continues to teach a course or a seminar at the Hebrew Union College in Cincinnati each semester. He also continues to produce important books in the field of American Jewish history. Though he tires and reluctantly takes brief rest periods throughout the day and evening, he gets to his desk by 9:00 a.m. and does not conclude his work-day until 10:00 p.m. This is his schedule six days a week, leaving only Shabbat for rest and renewal. His contributions to American Jewish life and letters, and his devotion to his students and his colleagues, make Dr. Marcus the best known and best loved Rabbi in the United States.

Jake Marcus is also a stubborn man. He has steadfastly refused to allow his biography to be written in his lifetime. He also refuses to write his memoirs. This book, then, is an attempt to preserve an intimate portrait of the man, and to glean from his writings a basic philosophy that emerges from commitment to the values and moral imperatives of the Jewish heritage which he cherishes with all his being.

To those limited goals of this book, Dr. Marcus agreed, and he willingly participated in many hours of recording his personal recollections on cassettes. He also insisted on personally editing the manuscript, so that the book reflects that which he wanted to share from his life experience with those who will read these glimpses of the man and his work.

Many persons were most helpful in gathering the material for this book and in preparing it for publication. I am grateful to the staff of the American Jewish Archives and especially to Kevin Proffitt, Archivist, for making available the biographical material and the photographs from their files. Dr. Stanley P. Cheyt, Director of Graduate Studies on the Los Angeles campus of the Hebrew Union College, has worked closely with Dr. Marcus over the years, and I thank him for his kindness in reading the manuscript and offering many helpful suggestions. I am also appreciative of the tireless efforts of Dr. Marcus' secretary, Etheljane Callner, and my secretary, Eva Wahl, who patiently typed and re-typed the manuscript as it came through several revisions.

My wife, Edna, shared with me the joy of living with Dr. Marcus in his home for a week, while we had daily sessions to record his oral history. She was, as always, an excellent sounding board, and a source of encouragement throughout this project. Most importantly, I am profoundly indebted to my beloved teacher and my cherished friend, Jacob R. Marcus, for allowing me the privilege of writing this book that offers some insights into his rich life experience, completely dedicated to his family, his students, and to the preservation of the priceless heritage of American Jewry.

RANDALL M. FALK

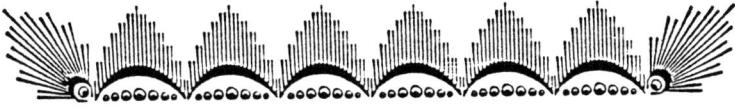

PRELUDE

I T WAS EVENING of the fifth day. As dusk descended Dr. Marcus lay back on his couch, weary from this final session of reminiscences. There was a faint smile on his lips as he spoke: "You know, I really didn't want to stir up old memories again. I was afraid it would be painful, that I would explore areas of my life that I prefer not to recall. But I've really enjoyed these sessions. The good times do outweigh the bad. I've been blessed in so many ways, and I'm grateful . . . very grateful."

Thus did we conclude the conversations between student and teacher, in which we sought to recapture relationships and events that have enriched Marcus' life. In some ways, his childhood was similar to that of untold thousands of children of East European immigrants who, arriving penniless on the shores of America, had by dint of hard years of struggle provided education and opportunity for their children. Many of these second generation American Jews were thus able to attain remarkable success in businesses and professions of their own choice. Some became famous, others accumulated vast wealth. It is safe to say, however, that few made a more profound contribution to American Jewry than did Jacob Rader Marcus—teacher and counsellor of hundreds of rabbis, and the scholar who established American Jewish history as a scientific study of the saga that began in 1585 with Joachim Gaunse. (Gaunse, a Bohemian Jew, landed on Roanoke Island in 1585; he was a mining expert sent over by

13

Sir Walter Raleigh to explore the mineral potentialities of the new country.) Marcus' many volumes on the history of American Jewry, and the Archives he established on the campus of the Hebrew Union College/Jewish Institute of Religion in Cincinnati are foundations upon which all future work in American Jewish history must be built.

At age ninety-eight Dr. Marcus continues the work that is the all-consuming passion of his life. He rises early, walks about a quarter of a mile with a colleague or a student, returns home for breakfast, takes a nap, and is at his desk no later than nine o'clock. He starts right in on his current project. His text is handwritten; he does not use a dictating machine until he has a draft. As a rule, Marcus works from nine o'clock in the morning until ten o'clock at night; he resents the loss of working time caused by naps he takes because he tires very easily. By ten o'clock he is ready to retire with a detective or western story and to sleep until 6:45 when he arises to begin another full day.

Jacob Marcus is not an uncomplicated personality; to appreciate fully the many facets of this man's character, we must understand his family background, his Jewish roots, and the Americanizing process to which he was exposed in his early youth. How fortunate I am to have shared my life with this man—to have served as his secretary for six years while I was a student at the College, and then to have been privileged to retain a close relationship throughout the next forty-four years. The week that my wife and I lived with Dr. Marcus in his family home, on what has been named Marcus Square by the city of Cincinnati, was invaluable in filling in some of the gaps in the story of his childhood and adolescence. Most of our understanding of this scholar-teacher, however, comes from his books and his lectures in which he sets forth his philosophy of life and his appreciation of the freedom which allowed him to live as a committed Jew and a proud American.

Now the memoirs begin!

14

1. THE FAMILY BACKGROUND

The saga of Jacob Rader Marcus begins in Russia, in the province of Kovno, in the town of Widzy (Vidzj), where both his father and his mother were born. In all probability the two never knew each other there, because they came from very different backgrounds. Jennie Reider (Rader) was one of the daughters of Isaiah Reider, who was called Shaye der doktor, or Isaiah the doctor. He was the village physician, trained through years of apprenticeship.

Aaron Markelson, Jacob's father, lived with his family a short distance outside the village, on a huge estate where his father served as steward. He probably oversaw the work of thirty or forty families for the Polish lord of the plantation. He was permitted to be a yeoman farmer on such a large scale because he had established himself as a farmer prior to 1882, after which no Jews in Russia were allowed to own or manage land in country areas.

Jennie and Aaron may have both come to America in 1889, but they took quite different routes. Jennie and her sister Dinah sailed directly to New York with their father. Dr. Reider had hoped to establish his medical practice in that city, but without a formal degree he had no future in the great metropolis. This disappointment, together with his immediate dislike for the way of life in this land, caused him to decide rather quickly to return to Russia. Dinah went back with him, though she soon married and returned with her husband to the States. Dinah and Zachary Melnik settled in Connellsville, Pennsylvania, outside of Pittsburgh and reared a large family. Many of Dinah's descendants are men and women of culture and distinction. Jennie, who had remained

15

in New York and was self-sustaining from the time her father left, visited her sister in Connellsville occasionally.

Aaron Marcus came to America after having completed five years of service in the Russian army. As a conscript, he was supposed to receive 45 kopeks, about 25 cents a day; the captain of his company kept his pay; Marcus never received any money. One of the few possessions he carried with him when he landed at Castle Garden, New York, was a watch which he had received as a prize for marksmanship while serving in a grenadier regiment in Russian Georgia. The grenadiers accepted only tall, well-built young men. After his release from the army, Aaron made his way to Hamburg, Germany, where he remained only a few months before obtaining passage to America. It was in Hamburg, too, that he obtained a new surname: Markelson was shortened to Marcus. The suggestion that he change his name was made by German Jewish acquaintances who thought that a change of name might make his way easier for him.

Aaron Marcus arrived in New York virtually penniless. He pawned his watch to pay for room and board until he got a job in a brick factory. He was a powerful man, but that job was too much for him. Aaron next went to work in a matzo factory, where he was exploited on a job that required his working 16 hours a day. He quit and secured employment as a sewing machine operator, after he had been given some training. However, he was fired the first day: he had sewn two right sleeves on a coat. Finally he had enough money to purchase a basket of notions, which he peddled all the way from New York to Pittsburgh, evading the constables who looked for unlicensed peddlers.

In Pittsburgh Aaron went to work in a small machine shop where he developed a good relationship with his boss, George Westinghouse, one of the founders of what was later to become a great industry. One day the boss came to Aaron and told him that he, Aaron, was going to quit. Marcus, frightened, asked Westinghouse why he was firing him. Westinghouse replied that he was not firing him, but that Marcus, being a Jew, would soon open his own clothing store! Eventually the prophecy came true. When Westinghouse had to close his shop for a time because he had fallen victim to the terrible financial panic of 1893, Marcus found another job in the Carnegie Steel Mills. He was discharged from that job when, trying to advance himself, he experimented with the operation of an overhead crane, which he almost destroyed. To make a long story short, he turned again to peddling and joined a number of other Jewish peddlers who made their headquarters in a village called New Haven, in Fayette County across the river from Connellsville.

By this time Aaron was married to Jennie Reider whom he met in Pittsburgh. Rabbi Sivitz, a famous Orthodox clergyman, officiated at their marriage. It was probably sometime in the early 1890's, and just about the time of the marriage, that he took out his first citizenship papers; he became a United States citizen around the year 1900. Aaron used some of his first savings to buy a gold Elgin watch which his son Jacob still carries proudly; the watch is over one hundred years of age and keeps good time.

Jennie and Aaron settled in New Haven, Pennsylvania. Their family soon included four children. The first son, Isaac, was born a year after the marriage. He was named for Jennie's father, the doctor. The second son, Jacob Rader, born March 5, 1896, was named for a brother of his mother who had immigrated to America and apparently disappeared. There were rumors that he had died in Detroit. In 1899 Jennie gave birth to twins, Frank and Ethel. Frank was originally named Raphael. Father Aaron the peddler had a horse which he admired very much by the name of Frank and it is very probable that the Anglo-Saxon name which he gave to his son was a compliment, not only to the horse, but also to the boy.

After the birth of the twins, Aaron briefly explored job opportunities in northeastern Texas, but what he perceived as the lawlessness of that region caused him to return to

Pennsylvania within the year. He told his son, Jacob, that he had seen peddlers being beaten up. In 1900 the family moved to Homestead, Pennsylvania, where Aaron, fulfilling Westinghouse's prophecy, opened a small clothing store.

2. THE EARLY YEARS

Jacob began his education in the public schools of Homestead at the age of six. He reports having been a slow learner, certainly in the first grades, probably because he was reared by immigrant parents whose first language was Yiddish; his English reading and writing capabilities developed rather slowly. In later years he found his knowledge of Yiddish a very valuable linguistic tool when he did research in the history of the East European Jews. It was Jacob's good fortune that his father believed very strongly in providing a sound secular and religious education for his children, for his sons at least; Ethel did not receive any formal Hebrew training.

Aaron Marcus had studied with a *rebbe*, a private teacher, in Russia, until he was thirteen years of age. He had a good knowledge of the Hebrew Bible and was particularly fond of the major prophets, whose social message appealed to him. This does not mean that Aaron Marcus had any leftist leanings; he looked with contempt upon socialists. He always voted the straight Republican ticket. Aaron had learned English in a few months of night school in New York City and could write a phonetic letter. He was determined that his children should have a better foundation for their lives. In order to encourage his son Jacob, he purchased a membership card for him in the Homestead public library, one of the first to be endowed by Andrew Carnegie, who was still alive. Though the youngster was only seven years of age, he frequently made his solitary way the half-mile from home to the library to return books and check out others. He was probably reading well by the time he was eight or nine. He still remembers that in order to go through the turnstile that admitted him to the young children's section, he had to allow his hands to be inspected to make sure they were clean enough to handle books. The boy soon became a prodigious reader. His early interest in history began with his fascination with the series written by George A. Henty. He read every book that Henty wrote and his retentive memory, inherited very possibly from his maternal great grandfather, a Talmudic child prodigy, became apparent at this early age and has been of inestimable value for him throughout his career.

It was in Homestead, too, that young Jake's *cheder* education began. This was a very pleasant experience. The Jewish community was Orthodox and it ran a respectable, well disciplined school to which Jake and his brothers went from about four in the afternoon until seven o'clock in the evening. The rabbi was scholarly and a gentleman. Jacob's older brother, Isaac, was a very serious lad. When the time came for the evening prayers he would stand up and recite them with dignity and devotion. One of the students, thinking he would have some fun, pricked Isaac in the buttock with a pin. Isaac flinched but continued his prayers until he had finished them, then very quietly—this was in winter—he went to the stove where he had left his skates, picked up one, and struck his assailant in the face almost cutting off his nose. After this episode no one bothered Isaac when he was reciting his prayers.

Jacob remembers the rabbi as the local omnibus factotum; serving as a *shochet*, a ritual slaughterer; he occasionally interrupted his classes to kill a chicken for a client, a member of the congregation. Later when the Marcus family lived down in Farmington, West Virginia—population: 800—Aaron Marcus attempted to keep kosher, killing his chickens, according to tradition, by cutting their throats. When young Jacob was delegated the job of dispatching a chicken, he took

Marcus, the Farm Boy in Farmington, West Virginia,
ca. 1914.

the ax from the barn and chopped its head off. Apparently even in those early years, he had already developed his own ritual code.

Public school and cheder education were not the only aspects of Jake Marcus' early childhood training in Homestead. The family lived in a poor slum area of the town, and some of his playmates ended in the state reformatory. He now recalls with horror that one of his fellow-students, who was only six or seven years of age, was confined in such an institution. He remembers also very well that once when he was going home from school—he was then in the first or second grade—he passed a bakery wagon and saw the back door open and no one around. There in full view was a large lemon pie that sold for a nickel. He didn't have the nickel, of course, so he grabbed the pie and ran. The driver spied him and chased him all the way home. There he insisted that Jake's mother pay the nickel for the pie. Of course Jake was punished for this theft—Aaron used a strap vigorously on Jake and his brothers when they needed correction. It was an age that truly believed in the axiom, spare the rod and spoil the child.

Another very interesting memory of Jake's early childhood concerned his association with a boy whose father was a carter for the Carnegie mills. Bear in mind that this was in pre-automobile days. This Christian family was very poor and the son would frequently steal soap from the outdoor washers where the mill workers cleaned themselves after their hard day's work. Jake was a confederate of this youngster. He also remembers that he had accompanied his friend to a drugstore where, when the pharmacist was busy in the back making up prescriptions, the boys would steal candies and chewing gum. This could have led to a life of crime, and unfortunately it did for some of his early chums. Jake learned, however, that crime was a double-edged sword. In 1904 his father gave him a bagful of campaign buttons advertising the candidacy of Theodore Roosevelt for president. Jake sold all of his stock in saloons and other places. When he returned to his father's store, prepared to gloat over the money he had earned, he reached into his pocket and found that his pocket had been picked. That day the eight-year-old lad said that henceforth he would live his life as a respectable citizen; his picaresque career was over. That did not of course mean that he would stop running with the gang to which he and his brothers belonged. The youngsters were not more than seven or eight years of age. He still chuckles as he recalls one Halloween night when some of the older boys in the gang used long poles to overturn outhouses. There was a man in one of the outhouses when the gang turned it over. Jake is sure the man would have killed any of the boys had he caught them; fortunately they could all run fast.

The youngster also had his first encounter with anti-Semitism in those early years. He and his family had gone on an excursion to visit the relatives in Connellsville. The train stopped in the station at McKeesport and the seven-year-old Jake stuck his head out of the window to look around. A group of boys were standing on the platform, and one of them shouted: "Stick your head back in, you God damned Jew!" Another indelible memory in the process of growing up!

The Marcus family moved to Birmingham, Pennsylvania, in 1906 or 1907. Birmingham is the south side of Pittsburgh on the Monongahela river. Jake ran with a rough gang there, too, and again encountered anti-Semitism — this time on the school playground. His older brother, Isaac, heard the big boys taunting the younger ones by calling them kikes and sheenies. Ike climbed the picket fence and attacked the fourteen-year-old bully who was frightening Jake and his friends. Young Marcus never forgot the pride he felt when his older brother came to his defense. While running with the youngsters, Jake discovered that there was a room in a nearby house that was full of books for boys. He went there and read practically every book in the library. It was only thirty or forty years later that he realized that this was a branch of a settlement house.

Jake walked a mile-and-a-half every Sunday across the bridge to Pittsburgh to attend the Sunday School of an Orthodox *Shul* whose leader was the distinguished clergyman Aaron Ashinsky. It was an excellent school staffed by young Jewish women who had gone to good universities. Here Jake received his first education in Bible and Jewish history. Back in Homestead he had merely learned to read Hebrew. One of his fellow students was Sol Feinberg, later not only a classmate at the Hebrew Union College but a close friend as well.

There is no question that the emphasis Aaron Marcus placed on education certainly influenced the youngster. Jake's father believed that learning was the key to success, to power; by the last decades of the century this is what more and more Americans believed as they turned to reading. Aaron Marcus, inveigled into a book auction house, bought a complete one-volume edition of Shakespeare for less than a dollar and brought it home to his four youngsters. The oldest was thirteen. The boys looked into it, found it incomprehensible, and importuned their father to return it. He brought back Horatio Alger's *Phil the Fiddler*, which they instantly devoured.

Ethel never had the opportunities the boys had, but years later when Aaron Marcus was willing to send his daughter to a convent school to further her cultural training, her mother refused to allow it for fear the daughter might become a convert to Catholicism.

The Birmingham sojourn for the Marcuses was brief. Aaron had opened a small department store in the town with high hopes, but approximately a year after he opened his business it fell victim to the economic panic of 1907 which destroyed hundreds of thousands of families. Aaron was forced into bankruptcy and left to seek a new home elsewhere. Because it was in the middle of the school year and Aaron was determined not to interrupt his children's education, he boarded them with a poor second-hand furniture dealer who fed the children and gave them mattresses to sleep on at night. This arrangement lasted for several months until the school term and the religious school year were over.

From Birmingham the family moved to Wheeling, West Virginia, where it was to remain for the next eight years. These were years that were to be especially important in molding Jake's character and in giving direction to the rest of his life. He entered the seventh grade of school in Wheeling, and by the time he reached the eighth grade he was the best student in the class. He was also the student with the best Jewish educational background at the Eoff Street Temple, the Reform congregation whose rabbi at the time was Harry Levi. Although father Aaron had helped found the first Orthodox Shul in West Virginia, where Jake became *bar mitzvah* at the age of thirteen, that synagogue had no cheder; thus, in order for Jake to continue his Jewish studies, he was sent to the Reform Sunday School in Wheeling, whose instruction left much to be desired.

The years Jacob spent at the Eoff Street Temple, which led to his confirmation there, were both personally difficult and tremendously significant in his life. The difficulty was that most of his classmates at the temple came from homes with a different social and economic background than his. The temple families were largely of German descent and they were already third or fourth generation Americans. Jake's parents, even though they had lived in the United States for many years, were still Eastern European immigrants; their Americanization was necessarily of a lesser degree. At that time East European Jews in Wheeling were often looked down upon by earlier Jewish settlers. In addition the Marcus family lived across the creek, an area occupied primarily by proletarian and lower middle-class citizens. After the confirmation ceremony, all of the children's families gave parties or receptions in their honor; Jake was not invited to any of them. Of course his family gave no party; it had no means. This bothered him a great deal and he never forgot the feeling of rejection. On the other hand, one of the wealthiest men in the Reform congregation took an interest in the youngster. This man's name was Kraft. Jake was impressed by the fact that Kraft had his own coach and driver. Occasionally he would drive over to Marcus' store where Jake worked after school, sometimes bringing him gifts; one was a gold stick pin that he has kept throughout his life. Kraft would talk to Jake on these visits and encourage him to continue his career as a student.

Mr. Kraft was not the only man in Wheeling who recognized that the youngster had a good mind and gave promise for the future. Rabbi Harry Levi, the son of East European Jews, was very fond of the youngster and was proud of the way he read from the *Torah* for the confirmation service. He had read the portion for that week in the original Hebrew. Shortly after confirmation Levi called on the Marcuses at their home and broached the subject of sending the youngster to the Hebrew Union College in Cincinnati to study for the rabbinate. In those days students entered the Hebrew Union College while they were still in high school. Aaron thanked the rabbi and said that he would consider his suggestion. The father discussed the matter with several of his friends, including an Orthodox Jew who traveled for a New York City Yiddish newspaper. The man said: "If you send your son to the Hebrew Union College he will become an apostate." Aaron also examined the *Union Prayer Book* in use at the Eoff Street Temple and pronounced it a "consumptive prayer book." This was typical of Aaron's keen wit, which Jake inherited. Aaron vetoed the idea of his son's going to the Hebrew Union College, so the family wrote to the Jewish Theological Seminary in New York, known in those days as Schechter's Seminary. The family received a reply from a young instructor there named Israel Davidson, who in later years became a scholar of great distinction. Davidson told the Marcuses that the seminary accepted only college graduates, and that if the boy was still interested he should get in touch with the college eight years hence. It was a curt note that discouraged Jake. When Harry Levi heard about this he again visited Aaron Marcus, this time pointing out that if Jacob went to the Hebrew Union College and graduated he could still become an Orthodox rabbi if he chose. Aaron finally consented, in part because his business was not doing well in Wheeling and he had no other prospects to offer his boy.

By this time the youngster, about fourteen years of age, was a skilled businessman. Jake had worked for his father since he was at least eight years of age and was fully competent to operate a men's clothing store. For centuries, in Europe, boys of thirteen had gone to work to make a living. When business was very bad in Wheeling, the youngster asked his father to give him some merchandise. He went to the local market house on the Sabbath, picked a booth, and tried to sell what he had. He sold nothing all day long. All he got from the day's work was embarrassment at being seen there by some of the members in his confirmation class. On another occasion, eager to help his father, young Marcus suggested that his father give him a pack of goods which he would peddle out in the country. But this project was a failure too. In later years Marcus recalled the fact that when they still lived in Homestead, and when he was only ten or eleven years of age, his father had to go to the market to restock his shelves. He left the youngster in charge. A customer came in and Jake sold him the most expensive suit in the store. He still remembers that the suit was a fine brown worsted. He fitted it for the man, and then proceeded to make the necessary alterations: he shortened the trousers. When his dad returned, Jake told him of the sale, expecting to be highly praised. His father simply said: "Good boy!" He took it for granted that the youngster could handle any business that turned up; otherwise he would not have left him in charge.

Despite an occasional success, Marcus grew up to hate

every aspect of the uncertain business world, although he had received excellent training. When the time came to matriculate at the Hebrew Union College in Cincinnati he left the store with few regrets.

3. TO CINCINNATI
AND HEBREW UNION COLLEGE

Young Marcus was fifteen years of age when he boarded the Baltimore and Ohio Southwest Limited train in Wheeling for the overnight journey to Cincinnati. Alone and frightened, the boy cried most of the way to Cincinnati. Had he known what lay in store for him—years of hard study—he might have cried even more lustily. The trip was broken by a stopover of several hours in Steubenville, where he wandered around the city taking in the sights. His worldly possessions were in a wooden and tin trunk in the baggage car. Arriving the next morning, he collected his trunk and took a nickel streetcar ride out to the College. The College had originally been housed downtown in the basement of the Mound Street Temple, the so-called vestry room. By the time that Marcus came to Cincinnati, the Hebrew Union College was housed in a large mansion, once a very beautiful private residence, on West Sixth Street, already in 1911 part of the West End slums.

Marcus rang the doorbell, and the custodian, whom Jake later learned the boys called the vice president, greeted him and directed him to take a streetcar to Avondale, the Jewish suburb, to see Dr. Morgenstern, one of the professors at the College. He found the professor, who was most courteous to him. Dr. Morgenstern had a list of boarding houses where the students lived. All of these places were the homes of East European Jews; not one of the proprietors was American-born and only very occasionally did a German Jewish family open its door to the students.

The first home to which Jake went did not work out; after only a couple of months the family decided not to continue

Jacob R. Marcus feeding chickens in the yard of his Parents' home in Farmington, West Virginia, ca. 1919.

to keep boarders. Perhaps hungry youngsters like Jake ate too much. His next home was in Mt. Auburn with an East European émigré family, who had been forced to flee Russia in the great expulsion from Moscow in 1891. These people were cultured Russian Jews who could speak Russian, German, and French. Jake remained with them for the rest of the academic year, though he was not happy there. He had not felt well most of the year. Though it was a fine family, and they were very good to him, he decided to make another move. He remained in touch with the family, though, and still visits one of the children, who is now a resident at one of the Jewish homes for the aged in Cincinnati.

Jake's third and final move as a student in Cincinnati was to the home of Mrs. Henry Reichman in Avondale. She was an illiterate woman, but kind and generous. Jake had never known a truly illiterate person before, but he became very fond of her and grateful for the three big wonderful meals she served every day, plus taking care of his laundry, all for just twenty-five dollars a month. He remained with her off and on for many years. Mrs. Reichman had two sons. One of them left school at sixteen and wound up as a mounted policeman on the Cincinnati Police Force. The other, Harry, was very talented as a singer and piano player. When Harry wrote to his mother, Jake would read the letters to her and respond. Though a widow who barely scraped by, Mrs. Reichman always managed to gather enough funds to send her son when he was in need. Eventually Harry changed his name and as Harry Richman became one of the most popular Jewish showmen in America.

One might wonder how young Marcus managed to have the twenty-five dollars a month for Mrs. Reichman, while he was a full-time student at high school in the morning and a Hebrew Union College student in the afternoon. The answer is that he came to Cincinnati with three hundred dollars in his pocket. His father had paid him twenty-five cents a week for working in the store since he was a child and that money saw Jake through the first year. Then things improved somewhat for his father, and Aaron was able to send the youngster funds during the second and third years when he needed them.

When the fifteen-year-old Marcus enrolled at the Hebrew Union College, he had finished two years of high school in Wheeling. His record there was anything but impressive. Of the five courses he had taken the first year, he had flunked two. He had difficulty with his English teacher, also, for she insisted that the themes he turned in were plagiarized: they were much too good to have been written by a boy of thirteen. The fact of the matter was that Marcus, a voracious reader, had already developed a vocabulary and a writing style that would have been a credit to a person several years older. Jake was also the best student in his history class.

His lackluster years in high school were due in part to the poor caliber of teaching in the Wheeling schools. Most of the teachers were graduates of Normal schools; they had received two years of training beyond high school. The principal, a Mr. Brill, was a Jew, a very fine gentleman. Marcus remembers him best because he constantly chewed tobacco, perhaps because Wheeling was the home of the largest chewing tobacco concern in the world.

Fortunately, Marcus' experiences in Cincinnati were quite different. The educational schedule for the seminarians in this Ohio metropolis was lengthy. They attended high school from 8:00 in the morning until 1:30 p.m.; then they pursued their rabbinic studies from 3:00 p.m. until 6:00 p.m. at the Hebrew Union College on Sixth Street. This continued for years, first at Woodward and later at Hughes High School on the hill; after the students were graduated from high school they attended classes at the University of Cincinnati in the mornings and at Hebrew Union College in the afternoon for the next four years. Throughout the years the students carried fifteen hours of academic work at the high school and later at the university, and fifteen hours of study at the Hebrew Union College. Dr. Kaufmann Kohler, who was then president of the College, had added a ninth year to the program so that the students would have one full year of rabbinic study and plenty of time to write their theses.

Marcus' academic record improved somewhat in Cincinnati. Whereas in Wheeling High School he had flunked geometry, in Cincinnati he made a high mark. In general, however, his academic work, both in high school and at the university, suffered because of the necessity of concentrating on the courses at the rabbinical seminary. In order to receive a scholarship at the College and a grant of $300 a year, the boys had to maintain a general average of 94. It is not surprising that the students concentrated on the grades at the seminary and gave little attention to their secular courses. Marcus' average grades at the university were an unimpressive 75 or 80. And yet, throughout his adult life, he has always worn a Phi Beta Kappa key on a chain across his vest. How was this possible? Did he purchase the key at a pawn shop as some are known to have done? Not Marcus. He was awarded an honorary membership in Phi Beta Kappa some twenty years after he received his doctorate in Germany and had begun to make a career as a scholar in the field of American Jewish history.

Jake's first year at H.U.C. was also difficult in many ways, even though Rabbi Harry Levi had taught him privately after confirmation. Jake read Hebrew fluently, and he had considerable training in the translation of the Pentateuch. Levi had also lent Jake a number of books; among them was Israel Abrahams' *Jewish Life in the Middle Ages*, a work which greatly appealed to him and probably helped set the course of his later academic life in the field of history.

However, because of Levi's training, Marcus was given advanced standing when he entered the College. He could not compete, though, with boys like Edward Israel, who was the brightest boy in the class. Julian Morgenstern, who was teaching the youngsters, called Marcus in and said, "Jake, I want to give you some advice. Go back to the first class and get a good foundation." The youngster listened to him and decided to do it, even though a friend in the second-year class, Jack Skirball — later to become a Los Angeles motion picture producer — urged him not to do it. But he went back with the understanding that he would be permitted to study over the summer, pass examinations in the fall, and rejoin his original class. In the first-year class there were some fine boys among whom he remembers Albert Minda and Ira Sanders best. They were inseparable. Albert was very friendly and a wonderful human being. He was quite a naive youngster, though, and at fifteen still did not know where babies came from. So Jake, who had been raised on the streets and in the slums of several towns, gave Albert his first lesson in sex education. Minda was shocked, horrified, disgusted, and Jake still chuckles and wonders some eighty years later: "Where the hell did he think they came from?"

Jake did not get along well with Ira, although decades later they became very good friends. His favorite term for Ira was "that so and so," and Ira felt the same way about Jake. Jake was particularly annoyed with Ira's mothering of Albert. In his high shrill voice, Ira would call to Albert as he crossed the street: "Be careful there, be careful, Albert." The three boys walked to high school every morning along with Abraham Shinedling to save the nickel streetcar fare, but returning home at six in the evening, dragging their rear ends, they took the streetcar. That is, all rode back home except Abe Shinedling. He had his shoes reshod with double soles so that he could save the nickel both ways. These young men learned the value of a few pennies the hard way. Jacob never forgot those early days of scrounging to make ends meet.

Sol Silverstein was a fellow roomer in the Reichman house and Jake thought of him as a rather wild lad. One day while Louis Reichman, the policeman son of the landlady, was asleep, Sol crept upstairs and took the revolver out of Louis' holster. Sol then came downstairs and started waving the gun around. Jake knew how dangerous this was—he had helped sell revolvers in his father's store in Homestead—so he grabbed it from Sol. As he did this Jack Skirball dived under a bed. Jack was embarrassed when he emerged and he said to Jake: "You bastard, you were too scared even to move." Jake laughed at him; guns never scared him.

There were good times and bad times in the boarding house. The boys shared common interests and goals which provided a foundation for friendships that continued over the years. When students went to a school for nine years they became close to one another, and when teachers taught students for a period of nine years they knew them inside and outside.

Young Marcus was a serious and able student at the College, though many of his teachers were poor pedagogues. Men like Moses Buttenweiser, who taught Bible; Gotthard Deutsch, who taught history; and Jacob Z. Lauterbach, who taught Talmud, had earned their Ph.D. degrees in Germany but had not been successful in obtaining university appointments there, primarily because of the prevalent anti-Semitism. These learned men found teaching elementary courses in a foreign language to young men who were ill-prepared to benefit from them very frustrating. Many of the boys were pranksters, Jake among them, and the tales of their practical jokes on their professors are myriad.

A year before Marcus came to the College, Professor Mannheimer, who taught Bible, had passed away. One of the legends that Jake's class inherited was about Mannheimer's sons, both of whom were students at H.U.C. In the springtime when youngsters were more interested in going to baseball games than sitting in class, Mannheimer's sons would decide to leave their father's class. They went to the window and dropped down four or five feet to the ground. The father saw them disappear and, not knowing how short the drop to the ground was, feared that the boys were committing suicide because he had been too stern with them. He shouted to them: "Don't kill yourselves, come back here." By this time, however, they had escaped and were on their way to a baseball game or to a stroll in the park. So the story goes.

One of the favorite antics in which Marcus frequently joined was called the feat of levitation. At a given signal all the boys who sat around the seminar table would raise their knees and lift the table very slowly off the ground. The professor — Buttenweiser — suspected what was happening and would duck his head under the table to see whose knees were raising it. By the time he looked under the table all the feet were on the ground and the table was back in its normal position. The professor was never fast enough to detect whose knees were responsible for this remarkable elevation of the table, particularly in view of the fact that all the hands were in sight on top of the table.

Marcus laughed the hardest, however, when he recalled how one of the boys would sneak out of the classroom about fifteen minutes before dismissal for the evening. This youngster would go to the restroom that both students and faculty shared. The toilets were in cubicles with batwing swinging doors. The lad would crawl under the doors — there was a foot of space — lock them from the inside, and then crawl back. When classes ended, the professors, for the most part older people, would rush to the restroom, only to find that all the toilets were locked. The students, of course, would go to the facility to watch the distress of the men who could not open the doors to the toilets. Marcus avers that the gyrations of the professors who where trying to restrain their full bladders until they could use the toilets was the real origin of the famous dance called the Charleston.

Despite all the fun, foolishness and high jinks, Marcus experienced tremendous intellectual growth during his student years in Cincinnati. His high school courses in Latin, Greek, and German, gave him some background for his later academic pursuits. However, never satisfied with his linguistic achievements, he felt he should have learned a great deal more. He graduated from Hughes High School in the spring of 1913 and the following year he enrolled in the University of Cincinnati where he was a student for the next four years. He had trouble getting into the university because he was short one credit. He had failed chemistry in high school because he knew no algebra; he had failed algebra back in Wheeling. In order to secure the necessary credit, he purchased a history of England, memorized the entire book, and passed an examination with a high mark. At the university he was particularly excited by the lectures of Merrick Whitcomb, who taught the history of the French Revolution. Marcus was impressed not so much by the content, but by the pedagogical approach of this man. In later years he was careful to pattern himself on this instructor whom he admired very much because he made his talks interesting. Marcus was of the opinion that if a lecturer is dull it is not due to the content but due to the manner of presentation.

In American history Jake did very badly. This was not because of the instructor so much as the fact that the work at the College was so exacting that he had no time to prepare adequately. However, he was fascinated by a course given by a man named Frank Wadleigh Chandler, who taught English. Under the tutelage of this man he read dozens of modern plays, which opened whole new worlds to him. He was always grateful for the experience of familiarizing himself with nineteenth and twentieth century drama. He enjoyed reading Galsworthy, Ibsen, Strindberg, and other notable European writers.

In 1915, while still going to the university (and of course to the College), Jake took a course in church history at the Lane Theological Seminary. There the "young Hebrew," as he was called, was one of the best students in the class, and, of course, some of his zealous classmates sought to convert him. He constantly found conversionist literature on his desk. He was not offended by this and his first experience of living closely with fundamentalist Christians was enriching; he learned to understand the nature of orthodox Christianity. This served him well in later years when lecturing to Christian clergymen.

However, it was at the Hebrew Union College, now located on its present site on Clifton Avenue, that Marcus began to experience his real intellectual growth. Henry Englander, the grammarian, and Julian Morgenstern, the Bible scholar, were teachers who challenged him in their courses. Marcus' favorite teacher was Englander, who was not only an excellent pedagogue, but was also a true gentleman and very considerate of his students. Jacob also admired Morgenstern, although his demands on the students were onerous. "Morgy" had been profoundly influenced by German pedagogy, when he was studying for his Ph.D. in Germany. This carried over into his teaching, without a decidedly negative impact.

Practically all the students liked Dr. Jacob Z. Lauterbach, who taught Talmud. He was always friendly and kind to the boys; they respected him as a scholar and enjoyed him as a human being. Lauterbach, a great student of folklore, was also personally very superstitious. He always led the *kiddush* on Friday night at the College dormitory. One night he was absent. The students looked for him. They found him outside the door on this Friday night refusing to go in because he was faced by a black cat. They heard him entreating the cat, "go away, cat, go away," but the cat refused to go away. The boys chased the animal away and Lauterbach rushed in and hurried through the kiddush ceremony. When the dinner was over, the boys turned to Dr. Lauterbach and asked, "How could you be so superstitious, doctor, a great scholar like you?" His answer? "I'm modern, I'm scientific, but vy take chances."

At the time Marcus came to the College, President Kaufmann Kohler, a very distinguished scholar, was known as being very absent-minded. As a result he was one of the professors on whom the boys played pranks. Kohler always called the roll in class using the current catalog which listed the students. The students delighted in taking a catalog which was ten years old and putting it on his desk before he arrived in the classroom. Obviously when Kohler called the roll, no one responded; Kohler would shake his head in dismay and begin his lecture.

The College's founding president, Isaac Mayer Wise, the great organizer of American Reform Judaism, had really not been a scholar. In contrast, Kohler, the graduate of a German university, had written a notable thesis; Wise had probably never had more than two or three years of elementary school training, but Wise built an empire; Kohler, in turn, distinguished himself by his learned writings: his book on theology and his articles in the *Jewish Encyclopedia*.

Of all of Marcus' professors, the one who had the greatest influence on him was Gotthard Deutsch. Early in Marcus' career he had begun to read the English translations of Heinrich Graetz's *History of the Jews*. Though Marcus' love of history dates back to the Henty books of his childhood, the Graetz work was the beginning of his intense interest in the history of his own people. This interest was deepened and expanded under Deutsch's tutelage. Marcus acknowledged his profound debt to Deutsch when he wrote in a brief unpublished autobiographical manuscript:

> He became a great influence on me. In part, he influenced me because of his personality. For the most part, I was influenced by his method. He was essentially a skeptic, a realist, a historical nihilist. He questioned much that appeared in print. He believed only in facts, and wanted to be pretty sure before he would accept a fact. He was in essence an annalist. He was also a great debunker. Deutsch emphasized the social aspect of history and was very much interested in details of the lives of individuals. I was profoundly influenced by this approach.

Jacob's positive experience at Lane Theological Seminary prompted him to go to the University of Chicago Divinity School during the summer vacation of 1915. There he was given a room for $8 a quarter. He supported himself by waiting on tables at the University Commons. It was his boast that he had spilled coffee on the best brains in Chicago. One of the highlights of the summer was the course in Egyptian history taught by the well-known scholar, James H. Breasted. Although Brestead gave enormous reading assignments which nobody could complete, he was an excellent lecturer. When, in later years, he wrote a history of the culture of the ancient world, he devoted only a few lines to the contributions made by the Hebrews. Judged also by his approach to the teaching of the biblical prophets, Jake realized that Breasted was no friend of the Jews.

During Marcus' years as a student he wrote for the *Hebrew Union College Monthly*. The student body magazine had been founded in 1914 under the editorship of an upper classman, Abba Hillel Silver, who later became one of the most distinguished rabbis in America. Marcus started writing for the *Monthly* shortly after it was founded. The final two issues of that first year included two book reviews by him. In one of them, a review of Israel Cohen's *Jewish Life in Modern Times*, Marcus criticized Cohen for allowing his Zionist zeal to interfere with his impartiality as an historian.

The next year Marcus, the author, received his first fee — $10 — from Joseph Jacobs, the editor of the New York *American Hebrew*, for an article about the famous East European Yiddish writer, Mendele Mocher-Sforim (Sholem Jacob Abramowitsch).

4. THE WAR YEARS

In 1917 Marcus, now twenty-one years of age, was made editor of the *Monthly*. His tenure in that position was short-lived. The United States declared war on Germany in April 1917. That same month Marcus enlisted in the army, though as a theological student he was exempt from military service. Fortunately he was stationed in Ohio with the state militia for a few months. He was thus able to complete his courses, take his examinations, and receive his B.A. degree in June, on schedule, from the University of Cincinnati.

Marcus admittedly did not enlist in the army primarily because he was a hot patriot, although he admired Woodrow Wilson tremendously. When Wilson spoke at Music Hall in Cincinnati in 1917, during his tour to propagandize for the United States entry into the war, Marcus was present, and since the crowd overflowed Music Hall, he was allowed, with many others, to occupy standing room on the stage. Though he was influenced by the president's speech, he was far more interested in Wilson's very attractive second wife, who was just twenty feet from him. He couldn't take his eyes off her. Finally she looked his way and smiled; she must have gotten his message!

If Marcus is confronted, he admits that he enlisted not only to make the world safe for democracy, but also from a desire for adventure. He always enjoyed wild-west movies — he still reads westerns — and he wanted some action in his own life. For the time being at least, he was burned out as a student. He had gone to college for about six years. Prior to that he had spent twelve years in public schools.

Since there were very few college men in the army — as a

Lieutenant Marcus, the Soldier in World War I, 1918.

matter of fact there were very few high school students—the newly-enlisted Marcus quickly found himself a battalion sergeant-major, one of the highest ranking noncommissioned officers in the regiment; he was assigned to the headquarters company. The tables of organization had been written during the Indian wars and technically Marcus was a mounted scout. Marcus' regiment, the First Ohio Infantry, orginally a militia organization, was sworn into federal service in the fall of 1917.

Marcus was not particularly happy during his early months in the service. There was a regimental senior noncommissioned officer who outranked him and set out to annoy him; there was also a former Y.M.C.A. director who was captain of a company and anything but a pleasant person. Jake was made uncomfortable by the anti-Semitic remarks that came to his ears. His first assignment was as secretary to the colonel of the regiment. He was required to learn shorthand, which he attempted to do in two or three weeks, but he was in no sense competent for this job. The colonel, Frederick William Galbraith, replaced him. Marcus was glad to be let off the hook. However, he retained his rank as a battalion sergeant-major.

After four months at the fairgrounds in Carthage (a Cincinnati suburb), Marcus was sent to Wetumka, Alabama, where he lived in a tent through the intense, bitter cold of the winter. He was with an interesting group of men, professionals for the most part. They all became good friends as they huddled in that tent during the cold winter months. One of his tentmates remained his good friend. He became an attorney and married the daughter of a Standard Oil magnate. Many years later Marcus went to visit his friend, who was now the father of a little girl. The child had heard that Jake Marcus was Jewish. When she was introduced to him, the first words out of her mouth were: "I don't like Jews." Jake never forgot that!

Marcus' regiment included a large number of boys of Ger-

43

man descent. As a matter of fact the names at roll call sounded so much like a German military outfit that at an opportune moment the regiment was dissolved leaving Marcus as a surplus noncommissioned officer. However, he retained his rank when he was assigned to the division's Judge Advocate-General's office, which handled court martials, criminal cases, and the like. The Judge Advocate-General was also in charge of the division stockade, which held soldiers incarcerated for criminal action.

When the troops were transferred to Wetumka for the winter of 1917–18, Marcus came in contact with many Jews. Whenever possible, Marcus conducted services for the Jews on Friday night. He also became the confidant and counsellor of many of the boys. One of the soldiers came to him and told him that he was going "over the hill," he was going to desert. Marcus talked to the lad, worked hard with him, and finally convinced him that if he went A.W.O.L. (absent without leave), he would give the rest of the Jews in the regiment a bad name. The boy did not desert. Marcus remembers also his conversations with another soldier, who in his determination not to go abroad where he might be killed, became a malingerer. The medical officer realized this and made the public statement that he was going to send that Jew to France no matter what happened. He went to France. As Marcus recalls:

> I met him years later after I had heard that he had played a heroic role. I said to him, "What happened to you, what did you do?" He said: "Well I didn't want to fight and I didn't want to be killed, but once I was in the army I wanted to show them what I could do and I was always in the front when there was a battle. My captain was always very careful never to let me get behind him. He had mistreated me and was afraid I might take a pot shot at him.

44

Marcus enjoyed helping his non-Jewish buddies as well. Most of the men stationed in Wetumka went to nearby Montgomery whenever possible. Some unfortunates returned with venereal diseases. Finally the chief medical officer of the division declared Montgomery out of bounds. A commissioned officer, a friend of Marcus', was one of many who sneaked out of camp and went to Montgomery to relax. He was caught and ordered to appear before a general court martial. Marcus and the Judge Advocate-General, determined to help the culprit, saw to it that those appointed to the court martial were friends of the officer. Fifteen minutes after the trial was held, the officer was exonerated. However, he could not be released from detention until the divisional printing office had published the decision of the court martial. This sometimes took weeks, Marcus solved the problem by taking the order of the court directly to the printer, waiting until it had been printed, and returning immediately with it; the prisoner was released forthright. In the army if you knew the ropes you could accomplish anything, Marcus discovered.

Inasmuch as Marcus was a surplus noncommissioned officer, he was removed from the Judge Advocate-General's office and reassigned to the Inspector-General's office, where to his distaste the young sergeant found himself spying on fellow soldiers. Somehow or other the news got out that he was looking for a new job. One day Willard O. Lathrop, the supply officer of the 145th United States Infantry, approached him and asked if he was looking for a new job. Marcus was only too eager. It took some finagling to get his release from the assignment with the Inspector-General, but he finally secured it and began a new life in the supply company of the 145th Infantry. He accepted demotion to a common wagoneer. This was in the days before the army was motorized. Later young Marcus became the regimental supply sergeant, the second ranking noncommission position in a regiment of 5000 men. Shortly before Jake moved to the

145th Infantry, former President Taft made an official tour of the base and came to division headquarters. Marcus noted that Taft was not interested in meeting with officers who had come up from the ranks. The former president was interested only in "Point" men, those who were graduates of West Point. Marcus' respect for the ex-president plummeted then and there.

The supply company which Marcus now joined was up to its full strength: a captain, two lieutenants, and about 250 enlisted men and noncommissioned officers. Jacob Marcus was the only man in the entire company with a college degree. That made all the difference in the world as he was ultimately to find out—army style. Meanwhile, one of his jobs as the regimental supply officer was to supervise the currying of about 300 mules. He rose every morning and made an inspection, as the soldiers in his outfit went about their work, to see that the mules were taken care of properly.

In the spring of 1918 the entire regiment moved on to Petersburg, Virginia, an embarkation center, where they were equipped for transportation to France and the battle-field. After a few weeks the supply company, along with about 10,000 men, boarded the old German *Vaterland*, probably the largest ship in the world. It was a hundred-thousand-ton vessel, a leviathan, and its name had been changed to *Leviathan*. The voyage across was a dangerous one and destroyers circled the ship day and night to prevent it from being attacked by submarines. Fortunately, they arrived at port in Brest, France, without any untoward incidents. The men disembarked and Jake's company proceeded with their heavy packs to march five miles up hill to their barracks. This was the most physically exhausting work that he had done since entering the army.

The next day the entire company was lined up, marched into Brest, and given the opportunity to buy liquor. When the outfit returned it was obvious to the young sergeant that many of the men were inebriated as the result of their excur-

46

sion. He vowed that as long as he was in France he would not touch a drop of liquor. He kept that promise.

It was not long before his outfit was ordered to the front, and the soldiers were deployed in trenches in a relatively quiet sector in the Vosges Mountains. The Germans were a mile in front of them. Inasmuch as Marcus was the regimental supply sergeant, he was stationed about a mile behind the lines. Because of the importance of his work he was treated with a great deal of respect, indeed, he had his own "dog robber," the term for a personal orderly. Among other things, the "dog robber" prepared Jake's "modest" breakfast every morning, which included a large steak and an ample supply of potatoes, coffee, and butter. Even Colonel Stanbery, who later became a general, treated the sergeant with a great deal of courtesy and consideration.

While in the service Marcus kept a diary. Once when he was typing a page for his diary another sergeant asked what he was doing. "I am doing a little typing," Marcus answered. The sergeant responded, "It looks like a diary to me. If you put my name in it and say anything about me I'll kill you." Marcus asked "Why should I put your name in it? I have no relationship to you." There the matter ended, but Marcus recorded the incident in his diary.

The 37th Ohio Division, to which the 145th Infantry belonged, was brigaded with an all-black division called the Buffalo Division. This was not a term of denigration. The name was given to it because buffalo have black, curly hair. Occasionally, the young supply officer had to take the train to an army base to secure supplies for the regiment. He would see that they were loaded on the train and he would return the same day. Once two black officers were on the train, seated close to him. A white soldier entered the car, passed the black officers, and ignored them. One of the black officers stood up, pulled his Colt .45 and said: "You salute me or I'll kill you!" The soldier saluted.

Marcus' division had moved up to the front to relieve the

77th Division, which was made up largely of Jewish men from New York's Lower East Side. For the first time since he had been in the service—and indeed for the last time as well—Marcus met two Jewish chaplains, Rabbi Elkan C. Voorsanger and Rabbi Benjamin Friedman; both were friends and older schoolmates of his. They were both very fine gentlemen. Of course there were other Jewish chaplains in the service, but most of them were in Paris or visiting the various Y's and other places where Jews congregated.

After several months at the front, orders came down from headquarters motorizing the entire division. Up to this time Jake had been responsible for animals—the 300 mules he cared for back in the States were replaced in France by Percheron horses. The new form of transportation was no longer wagons and horses but Nash trucks, and all men with any mechanical training were given promotions to higher rank. Marcus found out that his orderly, who had once been a fireman on a locomotive in civilian life, would now outrank him. When that happened he went to his captain and told him that he was now ready to go to an officer's training camp. This opportunity had been offered him frequently before, but he had had no interest; he enjoyed his job as a supply officer. Captain Lathrop, Marcus' immediate superior, arranged for him to appear before the selection board for an officer's training camp. Marcus arrived for the interview with his jacket improperly buttoned and his medical pouch on the wrong side. After chiding him gently the examining committee asked him but one question: Was he a college graduate? When he answered in the affirmative, his application was approved without further interrogation. He was obviously what the board was looking for, a "gentleman," fit to be an officer. Other candidates, men who were common soldiers, were bypassed; they had no educational background.

The young aspirant arrived at Fort Bonnelle in Langres, France, with seven hundred other candidates, for officer training. The major in charge of the camp was a Marine. Inasmuch as there was a necessity for a supply officer to provide for the seven hundred men, the major went through the list of all candidates who were regimental supply noncoms. The first two names he called did not respond to his call; they had gone to town to see the sights or to have a few drinks. Marcus was the third supply noncom on the list and he was given the job of making provision for the trainees. In addition, of course, he had to keep up with his studies and other requirements for officer training. The rest of the men lived in barracks; Marcus, as the supply officer, was given his own room. At night after "lights out" Marcus would light a candle, shield the cot with his blanket, crawl under the cot and study for the examinations. It wasn't long, however, before the major caught him violating "lights out" and made him stop. Nonetheless, Marcus passed his exam and was made a second lieutenant. He knew very little about army regulations and tactics, but he wrote a literate English. That was important. He was now a "shavetail," a second lieutenant.

Marcus fortunately was never required to lead a training platoon at the fort. The authorities left him alone, fully conscious of the fact that he was not adept in the area of "squads rights." One other candidate, an older person with a background similar to that of Marcus, was not so fortunate. He was given a platoon to lead and did everything wrong including marching his troops into a wall. Marcus was commiserating with him one day, and in the course of the conversation the man said that his name was James and he came from Massachusetts, from Cambridge. Marcus asked him if he was related to Professor William James of Harvard, and found out that indeed he was. The professor at Harvard was the man's father. This son of William James later became an executive at Harvard University.

When the candidates who survived the examination were commissioned, it was understood that they were to be sent to the front after the St. Mihiel and Argonne offensive against the Germans had started in September 1918. Toward the end of the month rumors began circulating that the Germans wanted an armistice. Marcus thought that this rumor was false inasmuch as the American army had not yet reached German soil. He bet heavily that there would be no armistice, but he lost his shirt. The Germans, after having virtually destroyed parts of France, ended the war before a single American soldier crossed their borders.

Marcus' division in the Vosges Mountains had its headquarters at Baccarat. His own company was stationed in Indian Village. When the time for the High Holidays rolled around, the New Year and the Day of Atonement, Lieutenant Marcus went to see the division chaplain, John Herget, a Baptist minister from Cincinnati. Marcus asked Herget to authorize the holding of services for the High Holydays. The chaplain was only too willing to do anything he could and made the necessary arrangements. Herget also secured the help of the Jewish chaplain in a French corps that was headquartered at Luneville and provided transportation for all the Jewish men in the division in order that they might meet at the bombed-out synagogue in Baccarat. Before the Rosh Hashanah services actually began, Marcus spoke to the men and asked them if they wanted a Reform or Orthodox service. Since most of the men were immigrants of Eastern European background they opted immediately for an Orthodox service. The French chaplain, who was of course Orthodox, was about to begin chanting the service when a lad from Pittsburgh whom Marcus knew very well stood up and demanded that the service be stopped inasmuch as the Scroll of the Law in the Ark was not ritually adequate, since the synagogue had been bombed and the Scroll had been neglected. Faced with this quandry, Marcus told the assembled congregation to wait while he consulted with some members of the local French community who were present at the service. With the little French that he had learned at the university he addressed the natives. He never knew whether they understood him. Nevertheless he returned to the congregation and very solemnly announced that the local Jews had assured him that the Sefer Torah was perfectly proper, kosher; they had been carrying on services since the bombing. The service then began. Marcus was determined that these men who had been assembled would not be denied the opportunity to worship together.

After the armistice of November 11, 1918, Lieutenant Marcus was put in charge of a large warehouse in Langres. The office had a relatively large staff and soon made it clear that Marcus was not welcome. The men in charge of the office had been without supervision for a long time. There was nothing he could do. When he realized what he had to face, Marcus walked out of the office and never returned; he devoted his time primarily to the administration of the warehouse itself. He had no trouble after that. At this juncture he learned the important lesson: don't beat your head against the wall.

Marcus was lonely, without friends or companions. He was eager to get back to his troops with whom he had been associated for well over a year, but army regulations made it clear that a man who had once been with an outfit as a soldier or noncommissioned officer would not be permitted to return to it after he was commissioned. It was his good fortune to make the acquaintance of an old army noncommissioned officer, a Russian immigrant who had reached the high rank of Master Sergeant. In those days a Master Sergeant was a soldier of great influence; many of these Master Sergeants had trained commissioned officers who later became commanders of divisions and army corps. One day while Marcus was taking a stroll through the streets of Langres he saw his friend, the Master Sergeant, talking to an officer. It would seem that the sergeant was negotiating a deal with a woman on the street. An army captain casting his lustful eyes on her was also interested. The captain turned to the sergeant and said, "move along, get going." The old

Master Sergeant, fully conscious of his power and his friends in high places, turned to the captain and said to him with his typical Russian accent: "You go to hell, she is poblic propiti." It was this man to whom Marcus expressed his desire to return to his former outfit. A few weeks later Marcus received an order returning him to his troops where he would serve as battalion supply officer. Obviously his Russian friend had used his influence with Chaumont, army headquarters in France. Thus for many months, until ordered to return to America, Marcus was back again with the supply company of the 145th United States Infantry.

When Marcus returned to his company he was also delegated to supervise the activities in a French village. Determined to see that sanitary conditions were properly maintained, he ordered his men to clean up a huge pile of cow manure. The peasant came out of his farmhouse, saw what Marcus and his platoon were doing, and started screaming in French: "It's my property, my property." Marcus desisted.

In May 1919 Marcus, as Acting Company Commander, mustered the supply company out of the service at Chillicothe, Ohio. He had served for almost two years and he had matured tremendously through his contact with a wide variety of men, under many different circumstances.

5. BACK TO COLLEGE AND CAREER

Marcus returned to the College as soon as he was released from the army. He used his wartime experiences for a number of articles he wrote around this time. Among them were: "The Jewish Soldier," *Hebrew Union College Monthly*, 1918; "Lost: Judaism in the AEF: the Urgent Need for Welfare Workers," *American Hebrew*, 1919; "Religion and the Jewish Soldier," *The Community Voice of the Allentown (PA) Jewish Community Center*, 1919. Marcus was now a senior and began to prepare for his ordination. To fulfill the requirements for ordination, he chose as his thesis subject: "An Investigation into the Polish Jewish Life of the Sixteenth Century with Special Reference to Isaac Ben Abraham, author of *Hizzuk Emunah*."

The other major undertaking for the senior year was a biweekly student pulpit. Marcus was assigned to Rockford, Illinois, but before he could go there he received a letter from the president of the congregation stating that he had already engaged a student for the year from the junior class of the College. The president had said that the young man had stopped in Rockford, met the president of the congregation, been invited to preach that Sabbath evening, and was offered the position. Rabbi Jerome Rosen, who was on the staff of the Union of American Hebrew Congregations in Cincinnati, was so indignant about this violation of College rules that he brought charges against the student. In this situation, however, as in most areas of conflict, the College faculty refused to take any action, even though the teachers knew that the junior was in no sense eligible for the position. So Marcus had

Marcus, the Horseman, ca. 1921.

no biweekly, no chance to prepare himself for the preaching rabbinate.

Marcus was not seriously discommoded by the lack of an assignment. He had come home from the army with a pocket full of greenbacks. It was only a matter of weeks before he had spent all of it entertaining the members of his class. It was pure accident that one of the students was not invited because he was not present when the invitation to go out and have a good time was made. The student found out that he had not been invited and was very angry. He happened to be a student teacher and when Marcus ran for president of the senior class he told the class that if Marcus was elected he would flunk everybody in the class. The election took place; Marcus lost. Years later this particular student became an intimate friend and associate of Dr. Marcus.

Finally, in December 1919 the pulpit in Lexington, Kentucky opened and Marcus was chosen to become the student rabbi. This was a fortunate turn of events because he not only was the biweekly rabbi of that city during his senior year, but he also remained its weekend rabbi for the two years before he went to Europe to study. Upon his return, Jacob served the congregation for four more years, now as a member of the College faculty. This was the only experience that Marcus was ever to have as a congregational rabbi.

When the members of the senior class became candidates for pulpits in the winter months of 1919-20, Marcus tried out for the congregation in Niagara Falls, New York, but decided he did not want to go there. He also tried out for the position of an assistant in New Orleans under the distinguished Rabbi Max Heller. Marcus was not, however, very eager to go into the congregational rabbinate; he was apprehensive, feeling that he did not have the capacity to serve as a competent rabbinical assistant.

Once when Marcus expressed some rather liberal ideas from his Lexington pulpit, some members of the congregation accused him of being a socialist. This disturbed him.

He did not like to feel that his freedom of speech was limited. In addition he did not especially enjoy speaking. As a matter of fact, the only aspects of his rabbinate which he looked forward to, were teaching the confirmation class and his association with the Jewish students at the University of Kentucky.

In the meantime, after his ordination, a number of people began to think of keeping Marcus at the school as an instructor. David Philipson, the rabbi of B'nai Israel congregation in Cincinnati, and one or two members of the College's Board of Governors, suggested to President Kohler that Marcus be appointed to the faculty. The faculty concurred and elected him as an instructor in Bible and rabbinics. Though the young rabbi's major academic interest was Jewish history, he was not appointed as a faculty member in that department. Gotthard Deutsch, the historian, though Marcus' friend, did not believe there was any need for another historian at the College. He had no objection if Marcus would teach biblical and post-biblical history; as far as he was concerned this was not "Jewish history." When Gotthard Deutsch died quite suddenly in the fall of 1921, the young instructor suddenly found himself teaching all nine history courses. Marcus managed to survive this formidable task by dividing the six-volume translation of Graetz's history into a series of segments and requiring the students in each class to read an assigned portion for the year. Actually the new instructor's most immediate contribution as a teacher at the College was that for the first time there was a systematic approach to the study of the history of the Jewish people, something that his predecessor with all his brilliance, and knowledge, had never provided.

Deutsch was truly a remarkable person but had a short fuse, and was easily angered. Once a student, determined to have some fun with the professor, asked him a legal question: "Can a man marry his widow's sister." Deutsch stroked his beard and started to think and finally realized that the boy was spoofing him. He picked up a huge chair, advanced on the student, and was about to strike him with the chair when he was finally restrained. After that nobody ever attempted to fool with Dr. Deutsch. It was too hazardous.

In addition to a very heavy teaching load, Marcus continued his weekend biweekly services in Lexington. On the whole it was a positive rabbinical experience for him, though he never felt comfortable working with the Board of Trustees. Once he asked for five dollars, not for himself, but for some project for the congregation, and the treasurer refused to give him the money. The rabbi never discussed money again until the end of the year. Then he went to Dr. Morgenstern, who was president of the College, and told him that the congregation was paying him but a pittance. Morgenstern agreed that the congregation was taking advantage of the young spiritual leader and suggested that he simply tell the members what he wanted, and what he believed he deserved. Marcus summoned his courage and told the congregational leaders that he felt his salary should be doubled. The congregation readily agreed; it was still paying him relatively little.

Marcus, the Athlete, ca. 1922.

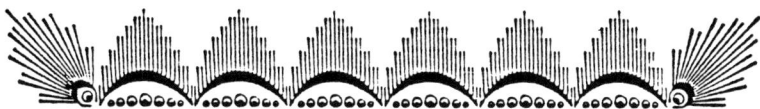

6. THE YEARS ABROAD

It did not take our instructor of Bible and rabbinics very long to realize that he was not competent to teach his classes. He was determined to go to Europe, specifically to the Lehranstalt, the Reform Jewish Theological Seminary in Berlin, a very famous and distinguished institution, to study and to prepare himself. In the summer of 1922 using the savings he had accumulated by his frugal life style — he had a walk-up cold water apartment for which he paid $35 a month — he left for Germany. The Lexington congregation presented him with an engraved Elgin watch, which he still prizes and wears.

Marcus did not leave his job at the College, but was given a leave of absence to go to Europe and come back with a degree. The College provided no funds or scholarship, but he did receive a letter from Morgenstern assuring him that his position would be available and he would be advanced in rank when he returned. Fortunately, Aaron Marcus had prospered in his move to Farmington, a tiny West Virginia hamlet, and by making real sacrifices helped his son during the four years that he pursued graduate studies in Europe. Today Marcus has a large picture of his father which he looks at constantly. They commune with one another. Marcus has always been of the opinion that we never really lose those whom we love; they remain enshrined in our hearts as long as there is a breath of life in our bodies.

Marcus went to Berlin primarily to study with the Jewish historian, Ismar Elbogen, at the Lehranstalt. He was not particularly happy with the academic offerings at this school, however, and so for the most part he continued his studies at the University of Berlin, at the time one of the very best schools in Europe. Here again he was somewhat disappointed, finding that the classes at the university were not up to the standards he had expected. As a result, he concentrated on private instruction in Medieval Latin, Talmud, and German. Fritz Baer was one of his tutors, and Marcus came to regard him as "technically, one of the greatest historians we Jews have yet produced." One of the great problems that faced the young rabbi in his first years at the university was learning to think and speak in German. He had no ear for language, and that plus the fact that his teachers at the Jewish seminary wanted to speak only English with him, made linguistic progress very difficult. So he decided to take a leave from Berlin for a semester and transferred to the university at Kiel where he did finally acquire the skill in German that he felt to be so necessary for his work. There he studied primarily with a distinguished historian who was one of the leaders in the production of the *Monumenta*, the great German series of works on medieval European history. Marcus did not work on the *Monumenta*, but merely attended lectures. At the expensive boarding house where he lived, he was amused rather than shocked to listen to the conversation of the people at the table who discussed quite seriously whether it was wrong to murder Jews in a pogrom. This was in 1923, ten years before Hitler came to power.

Jake was terribly lonely in Kiel, though he met a number of fellow Jewish students there, but for one reason or another he had very little in common with them. As soon as possible he returned to Berlin. His German conversation still left much to be desired: when he had joined a Turnverein and spoke to his fellow members in Kiel, they turned to him and said, "Your German is rather peculiar." With a smile he said to them, "Well, I come from Bavaria." They nodded solemnly; they understood why he did not speak the way they spoke.

He had some dear friends in Germany, among them a

cellist by the name of Maurice Eisenberg. He would frequently go down to Leipzig where Eisenberg was working and studying and spend the weekend with him. One of his problems was finding a synagogue that offered him a style of service that he felt would be inspiring or at least satisfactory. He attended an Orthodox synagogue and it left him cold; he went out to hear the famous Dr. Leo Baeck, but Baeck, though a magnificent human being, was not an entrancing preacher. He wandered one day into the left-wing Reform synagogue on Johannisstrasse, but found this so lifeless that he left before the service was over. Occasionally he went to a Chassidic service in the heart of the Jewish ghetto and enjoyed it. Finally he went to a traditional service conducted by right-wing dissident Orthodox Jews. He enjoyed it tremendously. The music was good, the preacher was brilliant, and Marcus was only too happy to be able to submerge himself in the traditional prayer book. When the High Holydays came around, he paid a very liberal fee to attend services, but when the congregants asked him if he was a traditional Jew, and he said he was not, they made a note of it, and he never received an invitation to mount the reading desk and to participate in the reading of the Torah. To these people, this young American was definitely not kosher. Marcus was never a "highbrow"; at that stage of his life he preferred the "schmaltz" of Orthodoxy to the sepulchral elegance and restraint of a decorous Reform service.

Marcus' loneliness was relieved in the summer of 1923 with the arrival in Berlin of Sheldon Blank, Nelson Glueck, and Walter Rothman, who had all been his students in history classes at the College the year before. He was only a year older than they, but he still felt a sense of responsibility for them. He looked upon himself as their mentor. He enjoyed their company, but soon found out that they were interested primarily in having a good time; apparently they had not come over to Europe to advance themselves academically. Somewhat pompously, Marcus called them to his room and lectured them on the opportunities that they were wasting. He urged them to settle down, work toward a Ph.D. degree as he was doing, and prepare for their future careers. He was sure that he had not influenced them to any degree, but much to his surprise and gratification a few weeks later he discovered that they had all signed up for courses and were hard at work.

It was about this time, too, that Marcus began dating Nettie Brody, an American girl from New York City who was studying voice in Berlin. He had gone on a blind date with Rothman and Blank and some American girls who were visiting in Berlin. Nothing really happened at this time but three or four months later he and Nettie started going to movies together. Marcus thoroughly enjoyed action movies as did Nettie. This was Marcus' first real dating experience. There had been a beautiful girl in Cincinnati whom he had occasionally walked home. She was Orthodox and did not ride on the Sabbath. She was European born, had only gone to night school, and her English left something to be desired. Marcus was fond of her and she was attracted to him. Nettie, however, was his first real love; they started dating in 1923 and two years later they were married on the eve of the new year. Marcus had hesitated to get married. He was a responsible person and the only warranty of his ability to support a wife was his letter from Dr. Morgenstern assuring him of his position and promising a promotion when he returned with his doctorate. Nettie saw no reason to wait; she had more confidence in Marcus than he had in himself.

Nettie and Jake were married in Paris because they could not afford to get married in Berlin. There were too many friends there who would have to be invited and neither Jake nor Nettie could afford a big wedding and reception. Marcus was barely eking out an existence as a student with help from his father, and Nettie was also living on a monthly check from her parents. Nettie's father, Joseph M. Brody, was a builder. A Russian immigrant, Brody worked his way through college receiving not only a degree as a civil engineer, but a Phi Beta Kappa key, too. He was highly successful in the building industry, but all that would be wiped out in the years of the Great Depression.

If the marriage in Paris was an effort to escape a large crowd of friends, the attempt was a failure. Nettie's family, more than fifty of them, came to the wedding in Paris. Many of them were Russian refugees; they were all people of education and culture. Marcus enjoyed their company. Marcus' best man was Nelson Glueck. Years later Glueck was to emerge as one of the great Palestine archaeologists of his time, with his picture on the front cover of *Time* magazine.

The officiant was Rabbi Maurice Liber, a prominent Parisian spiritual leader and the author of a well-known book on Rashi. Immediately after the wedding, Nettie went back to Berlin to continue her music studies, but Jake had decided to remain in Paris to further his knowledge of French. A week after Netttie returned, Marcus sent her a telegram: "Can study French in Berlin as well as in Paris. Am arriving on the next train." They continued together in Berlin until the spring of 1926 when Marcus left for Palestine determined to learn some modern Hebrew.

Jake was very disappointed in this, his first visit to Palestine. The only place where he could readily learn modern Hebrew was on a kibbutz, but life was simply too primitive for him there. He had studied intensively for almost four years in Germany and was very tired. Although Marcus had always lived frugally, he knew he could not adjust to the environment of a Palestinian kibbutz in 1926. He spent a few months in Palestine living in the American School of Archaeology, learning to read a modern Hebrew newspaper, and fighting the sand fleas. He was fortunate there was enough water in the American school to take a shower once a week. Two-and-a-half months after his arrival, Marcus left to rejoin Nettie in Marseilles; she had come down to meet him. Following a brief second honeymoon in France, they booked passage on a ship and sailed for America.

Marcus, the Mountain Climber at St. Moritz, Switzerland,
December 1924.

7. RETURN TO H.U.C.

In the fall of 1926 Marcus was back at work at the Hebrew Union College, as an instructor. His promotion had not come despite the fact that Marcus had earned his Ph.D. degree magna cum laude in Berlin and his dissertation, *Die handelspolitischen Beziehungen zwischen England und Deutschland in den Jahren 1576–1585*, had been well received and published in 1925 by Eberling in Berlin. It was dedicated to "Pretty Nettie Brody."

When, after seven years, Marcus did not receive a promotion, he turned to a dear and much admired friend, Dr. Rosenau, a rabbi in Baltimore. Rosenau was a very influential member of the Hebrew Union College Board of Governors. He saw to it that Marcus received his promotion. It took him several more years before he gained the rank of full professor. Later the chair that he occupied was the Adolph S. Ochs Professorship of Jewish History, and when he turned to American history the chair became the Adolph S. Ochs Professorship of American Jewish History. Ochs, of course, was the distinguished publisher of the *New York Times*. In 1965, Jake became the Milton and Hattie Kutz Distinguished Service Professor of American Jewish History. Mrs. Kutz, who endowed his new chair, was the widow of a vice president with the DuPont corporation in Wilmington, Delaware.

The doctoral degree was not all that Marcus brought back from his years abroad. He had become a cultured person through his association with musicians and artists. More important, he had accustomed himself to the disciplined demands of scientific scholarship, which made the rest of his life highly creative and productive.

Nettie was very patient with all the demands that Marcus' profession made on both of their lives. Her gaiety and social affability were fortunately able to lighten her husband's intensity and even his hyper-sensitivity about his status in the Cincinnati Jewish community. He could never forget that he was the son of Russian immigrants in modest circumstances, and he had reason to feel that the German-Jewish elite of Cincinnati was not always receptive and cordial. Of course he may well have exaggerated the social distance that existed between him and the laymen who were associated with the College community. His sensitivity was reinforced by an incident that was repeated to him by a matron of the Hebrew Union College dormitory. When the son of a very distinguished club-woman married out of the faith, the matron of the dormitory expressed her regret in a conversation with this prominent Jewish social leader. The woman responded: "Yes, but thank God it wasn't a Russian Jewess."

Five months after Jake and Nettie had settled down in Cincinnati, Nettie returned to Germany for additional studies in preparation for a concert that she hoped to give. Jake missed her, but never questioned her desire to make a career for herself. He made every possible effort at all times to further the career of his wife. After returning from Germany where she had given a concert, she sang and taught music and filled her life with her work and her social companions. She was a fine pianist, and a good if not exceptional singer. She enjoyed teaching and was devoted to her pupils. Nettie was also an excellent bridge player and almost every night she had a bridge game at their home. She tried to teach the game to her husband, but he was not interested and never learned to play any card game. At the end of the evening when the game was over, she always served a collation. She would then call up to him to come down—his study was on the third floor. He always came down, enjoyed the repast and socialized briefly with the guests. Nettie and Jake were devoted to each other; he was appreciative of all that she had done, particularly teaching him the amenities that he had never learned at home.

Despite her frequent illnesses Nettie managed to run the house efficiently; she was a superb cook. She continued to be her husband's hostess for many dinners in their home. The boys always looked forward to these occasions, and especially to the annual seders to which the Marcuses invited them. Jake was truly in his element as he led the seder. He and Nettie invited as many of the students as the dining room could hold and they sang, read the Haggadah, and told stories late into the night.

The Marcus' only child, Merle, was born in 1929. Merle was the apple of her father's eye, but, although he did everything humanly possible for her, spoiling her in the process, the two had different temperaments and tended to live lives of their own. While Merle was still young, Nettie's health began to fail. She passed away in 1953.

Merle was determined to have a career on the stage; she did have a good voice which enabled her to appear in some light operas and other summer theatre productions. Tragically, she died in Los Angeles just as her career appeared to be taking off. While Marcus had finally become reconciled to the passing of his wife, he never really has gotten over the early loss of his only child. After her sudden death he was sustained spiritually and emotionally by his brothers and his sister, and by his many friends at the College. His extended family, throughout his years on the H.U.C. faculty, were his "boys" who had been his students.

Over the years Marcus became the favorite teacher of many students. He maintained a friendly relationship with most of them; they respected him and found him an understanding and compassionate mentor. His "boys"—many now retired—fill rabbinic and academic posts throughout the world. During the first decade of his teaching career, he offered a wide variety of courses in addition to history: Bible, some rabbinics, and a course in customs and ceremonies. He was a good teacher, exacting and thorough in his preparation. He expected the boys to prepare for his classes and regularly examined them on their reading. In all his history classes, except for the advanced seminars, Marcus gave a ten-minute written quiz at the beginning of every session. He also required book reviews, which he read very carefully. This involved considerable work for both the students and the teacher. He always demanded a great deal of himself and expected no less from those who came to his classes.

From the first year of his teaching career, Marcus especially remembers his friendship with Sidney Regner and Herman Snyder, both of whom remained dear friends throughout the years. Babe Glaser was another student whom Marcus remembers well. Glaser was later to become an assistant rabbi in Pittsburgh and New York and ultimately the chief liberal rabbi in Detroit. One semester Glaser was the only student to register for a course in the Book of Numbers. The entire book was read in the Hebrew. Marcus was only too happy to give a course for one student. In their first class session, Glaser read for thirty minutes and, becoming hoarse and tired, turned to the instructor and said, "Doc, now you read," and Marcus read for the next thirty minutes. That was the pattern they followed during the entire semester. Both men learned a great deal in the process. Martin Weitz was another of the students with whom Marcus established a warm friendship in the early days. Martin would walk Jake home many afternoons, after classes were dismissed for the day. The two men talked at length about their shared interests and aspirations.

Marcus' first real disciples and intimate friends were Allen Tarshish and Sam Sandmel. Marcus took Sam Sandmel under his wing and made every effort to help him over the rough spots. Their closeness grew over the years, and in their daily walks they discussed many aspects of their lives and the problems that faced them. Sandmel had respect for the common sense that always characterized Marcus and turned to

68

him with academic problems and challenges. In turn, Sam was a tremendous support to Jake during the two over-whelming tragedies in his life: the deaths of his wife and his daughter.

Bert Korn was another of Marcus' close disciples, one of the first to follow his mentor into the field of American Jewish history. Jake affectionately named his student "Pop," when he found out that his name was Korn, and the relationship became even closer after "Pop" was ordained and became an assistant to the president, Nelson Glueck. Most nights after working together on some aspect of American Jewish history, the two would go out for hamburgers. Marcus loved to keep up with the latest "gossip" about what was going on in the rabbinate: pulpit vacancies, Central Conference of American Rabbis politics, activities in the Union of American Hebrew Congregations and at the branches of the College in Los Angeles and New York. Until the Placement Commission was created by the C.C.A.R., the U.A.H.C., and the H.U.C.-J.I.R., Marcus was active in placing rabbis. He was widely known in congregational circles because of his popularity as a lecturer. Presidents of congregations frequently turned to him for recommendations of candidates for their pulpits. Rabbis seeking assistants also sought his counsel. Naturally he was most helpful to those who were close to him, but he was always honest with colleagues, presidents, and personnel committees. He effectively arranged "marriages" between congregations and rabbis.

It is interesting that Bert Korn, Dr. Marcus' disciple, became Nelson Glueck's assistant. A number of Jake's stu-dents wondered why he never became the president of the Hebrew Union College. In May 1947, after it was announced that Dr. Morgenstern was leaving, a search committee for a new president turned to Marcus and met with him in the board room of the Hebrew Union College. When he found out that the committee members were willing to consider him, he replied, "Thank you for thinking of me, but I am no candidate for the presidency." He had known before he went into the board room that he had a decision to make. He knew that if he became the College president he would cease to be a scholar. Without any hesitation he made his decision and he has never regretted it. The members then asked him whom he would recommend. They presented a slate of half a dozen men and he discussed these names with them very frankly. Marcus insisted that Nelson Glueck was the best candidate. They told him that they had offered the position to Dr. Glueck several times, but he had turned them down. When Marcus heard this—he was Glueck's oldest friend—he said, "go back once more and insist." They went back, they insisted, and Glueck accepted.

Another one of Marcus' disciples was Stanley Chyet, who earned his Ph.D. under Marcus. Chyet, like Korn, was completely devoted to Marcus and has made his own mark in the field of American Jewish history, first as a member of the faculty in Cincinnati and later on the Los Angeles campus. No matter what Marcus writes, he always sends Stanley his manuscript to vet for him. He has never been disappointed. Chyet has a fine background both in Jewish history and in American and English literature and an unusual understanding of the nuances of the English language.

Over the years Marcus has had many student secretaries who assisted him with his personal correspondence and his work when he first organized the American Jewish Archives in 1947; all remain close to him. The College had a student employment program called the Placement Bureau. The authorities always turned to Marcus when it was necessary to find work for students; he never failed them. When he began the Archives, he employed all those students who sought work. When five German refugee students came to the College, they were put to work scouring the outstanding European Jewish newspapers for items of American interest to be filed at the Archives. All five students graduated and became notable American rabbis. Among the secretaries who worked for him and became his intimate friends were Byron Rubenstein, Eugene Lipman, and Randall Falk. As the College became more prosperous, the institution provided Marcus with professional help. The ties, however, that the student secretaries enjoyed with him in the early years of the Archives are cherished by those who are still living. They keep in constant touch with him.

The depression years brought additional problems for Marcus. His father died in 1933. Following his death, Marcus and his brothers found it necessary to support their mother and their sister. Financial responsibilities, both at home and for his family who lived in Pittsburgh, were prime reasons why Marcus spent so many weekends traveling to congregations throughout North America delivering lectures on a variety of subjects. In the course of his lecturing he discovered that his talk, "An Old People in a New World: The Romance of the American Jew" was always well received. Marcus facetiously called this talk "22B"; he still uses it. In addition, Marcus was frequently called upon by congregations to lecture at Institutes for Christian clergy. These occasions were concerned primarily with Jewish-Christian relations. Marcus' excellent memory for people and events, his delightful anecdotal style, and his personal warmth have made him a popular speaker throughout his career. At the age of ninety-eight he is frequently invited to speak, but he has limited himself primarily to speaking engagements in the environs of Cincinnati.

One of the secrets of his success on the lecture circuit is that he always has been meticulous in his preparation. He never ceases being nervous before departing for a speaking engagement, but when he begins to talk no one ever suspects that he is tense. He speaks fluently and with an innate charm that enables him to hold an audience. In discussing speaking engagements with his students, he would never fail to grade himself on his last lecture. He has seldom given himself a grade of more than 90, rarely in the 90's, and never

100. He maintains that no person is perfect. For that reason also, he almost never gave a student the top grade of "E" on a term paper, a book review, or as a semester grade.

Despite the fact that Marcus was a demanding teacher, whose course requirements were heavy, and whose standards for book reviews and term papers were high, his students respected him as well as had a genuine affection for him. They recognized that he taught them much besides history.

At the beginning of their freshman year and at the end of their senior year, Marcus always gave an address to the class interpreting the role of rabbis in congregations and in their community. He discussed standards by which he felt a rabbi must live and what he felt it was that made for a good and decent rabbi. His students listened to him intently as evidenced by the testimonials they wrote in a tribute volume, *Biz Hundret un Tsvantsik!*, edited by Abraham J. Peck and Jonathan D. Sarna, on the occasion of Marcus' ninetieth birthday.

It is impossible to include all of the wisdom gleaned and sentiments expressed in these outpourings of gratitude and love from Marcus' students. A sampling of them, though, gives us some insight into what his students found most important in the lessons learned from their mentor.

Malcolm Stern, another of Marcus' proteges in the field of American Jewish history and genealogy, enumerated seven lessons he had learned from Jake Marcus. The first and the last are most interesting: "History is not names, dates, and places, but the record of human beings responding to their environment," and perhaps the most fundamental Jewish history lesson of all: "Never a first Jew anywhere; there's always one who got there ahead of him" (p. 73).

In quite another vein, David Polish, one of Marcus' earliest students, highlighted his mentor's strength of character: "Above all, Jacob Marcus has set an example for transcending adversity and for confronting it with creative courage . . . all of us marvel at his use of wit and humor as a weapon against despair. After all, this is one of the epic lessons of Jewish history" (p. 57).

One of Marcus' more recent students, Lewis Kamrass, summarized the lessons for life that his teacher had transmitted: "Always prepare carefully and thoroughly. Keep your integrity at all times. Be a gentleman to everyone, and, remember to laugh: to view the world, your work, and yourself with a smile." To which Kenneth Kanter adds: "Another precious value is humility. . . . Dr. Marcus reminds us that we are as good as our last sermon, speech or book" (p. 27).

Alvin Rith summarized the impact of Marcus' close relationship to his students when he wrote: "Dr. Marcus raises up disciples with joy, spurs them to goals beyond their own perceived strengths, comforts them in their defeats, and rejoices in their victories as though they were his own. In fact, they are" (p. 63).

Colleagues on the faculty also wrote of their gratitude and their admiration for Marcus. In his introduction to the tribute volume, Alfred Gottschalk, president of the College, wrote:

> Early in his career, Dr. Jacob Rader Marcus said, "Books are the memory of mankind. A people that is not conscious of its past has no assurance of its future." These words reflect well the man and his work. . . . Dr. Marcus is the memory of American Jewry (p. 2).

Michael A. Meyer, a fellow historian at the College, captured the essence of Marcus, the scholar, in this summation:

> What I have learned above all from Jacob Rader Marcus is to appreciate the rigor of *Wissenschaft des Judentums*. Marcus, the scholar, has enabled me to recognize how very important is the scientific approach to research and writing. He had taught me both the necessity of

73

honesty and distance in dealing with historical sources and the need for extreme care in achieving the maximal degree of accuracy even in the smallest of matters. From Jacob Marcus, the man, I have learned that scholars can also be gentlemen (p. 50).

To this latter statement, we would add the words of a younger colleague, David Weisberg, who epitomized the feelings of all who know Jake Marcus, when he wrote: "The most memorable thing about him is very simple: There's not one phony thing about Dr. Jake" (p. 81).

Samuel Sandmel probably knew Marcus best. He was first a student, then a colleague, and especially in the latter years, until Sandmel's untimely death, Marcus' confidant on their almost daily walks. In a brief essay in *The Writings of Jacob Rader Marcus*, a bibliographic record compiled by Herbert Zafren and Abraham Peck, Sandmel provided a portrait of the man that helps us understand better this unusual scholar and teacher. Sandmel wrote in part:

> His devotion to scholarship can be indicated in a few words: scholarship is his vocation, and is also his avocation. Scholarship is his work, and scholarship is his pleasure. Nothing easily diverts him. His attendance at faculty committee meetings has not been an unbroken pleasure for us, his colleagues, because normally the meeting begins with his taking out his pocket watch and indicating at what hour and moment he will depart from the meeting, whether the business is completed or not. He would much prefer not to serve on a committee than to serve. In serving, he would rather be chairman than merely a member, because he has thought that as chairman he could control the length of the meeting (possibly even the substance). Why this attitude to committee meetings? Because they interrupted his scholarship. There is a great paradox in all this. . . . Those knowing him only socially, and admiring his

geniality, his sense of humor, his warmth, are never quite ready to believe my accounts to them of a man who works at scholarship morning, noon, and night. Such people see nothing of a misanthrope about him, as they correctly describe him as congenial and convivial. Yet, let him be out to a dinner party, and the life of the evening, and one can be sure that around 9:30 or 9:45, he will announce that it is time for him to leave and to return to his study and thereafter to put in another hour or two on his writing. This is his standard operating procedure.

Does he sound like a single-minded man? In one sense he is. Yet the same single-minded man has an unbroken record of never turning down a student who wants to see him. For students his time is freely available. To requests that have come to him from the community and its manifold organizations, he has had no difficulty in saying no. But should an identical request come from a student . . . then he is certain to answer affirmatively. . . . What is he dedicated to beyond his own scholarship? It was he who more than anyone else turned the study of American Jewish history from filiopictism into an academic discipline. It is academic productivity as a requirement for all scholars that is the hallmark of what he stands for.

Before immersing ourselves in Marcus' literary contributions, one other area of his impact on the Reform rabbinate must be disclosed. Jacob Marcus was, in every sense of the word, the rabbi's rabbi. Long years after his "boys" and later, "girls," left the College, they continued to turn to their mentor for advice and guidance.

Bert Korn expressed it best in his Founders Day address on the Cincinnati campus in 1976, when Marcus was honored by the College on the occasion of his eightieth birthday. In the course of the address Korn said:

As a matter of definition, no rabbi is a fool. But even the best of rabbis gets himself involved in some darn fool problem. Dr. Marcus has probably heard every story there is to tell about a rabbi's situation, but he still listens with infinite caring, and guides his inquirers with all the shrewd sharpness developed in his Litvak ancestors' bitter struggle for survival. This is one of the many incredible things about this man: he has never served a congregation [that is, as a full-time congregational rabbi] but he knows more about congregational and communal life than all of the authorities put together. He has pursued the best face-saving device through the intricate corridors of so many mazes that he can draw the diagram of a solution better than the best novelist. It is the quality of warm helpfulness that continues to draw so many hundreds of his students to him over the telephone, at meetings, and especially at the annual conventions of the Central Conference of American Rabbis, which paid him the high honor of electing him President [1949–50], the first Hebrew Union College professor since Isaac Mayer Wise himself, to serve in that important office (Korn, "Cry Out in Joy," pp. 6–7).

It was typical of Marcus that he chose to serve as president of the Conference for only one year, though a two-year term was customary. He had hoped to set a precedent of one-year terms, so that more rabbis would have the privilege of serving in that office. Unfortunately, he was not successful in changing the Conference election pattern. In 1978 the Central Conference of American Rabbis elected him as its Honorary President. He maintains that this is the highest honor he has ever received, and the one he cherishes the most, even in the face of several honorary doctoral degrees and other distinctive forms of recognition.

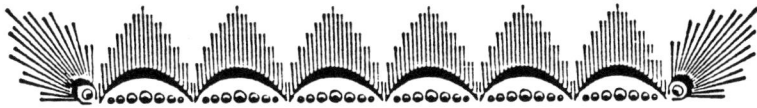

8. THE LITERARY HARVEST

In order really to know and appreciate Jake Marcus, his wisdom and his philosophy, we must turn now to his books and essays. *The Writings of Jacob Rader Marcus: A Bibliographical Record* lists two hundred and twenty-three items written by Marcus between 1916 and 1978. Of course, the past thirteen years have seen many significant additions to this list, the most important of which is his four-volume magnum opus on American Jewish history. The first three volumes have already been published by Wayne State University Press. The final volume has been completed by him and is awaiting publication by Wayne State.

Interestingly, Jake's first published article was "America: The Spiritual Center of Jewry." It appeared in *The Jewish Community Bulletin* of Wheeling, West Virginia in 1916 when Marcus was twenty years of age. It was a prophetic forerunner of the field to which Marcus would devote himself in his writings and in his founding of the American Jewish Archives. The article also anticipated the basic philosophy which impelled him to concentrate on a scientific study of American Jewish history: that European Jewry and its great centers were in decline or danger, and that America would become the spiritual and political focal point for World Jewry.

From the first, Marcus' work has shown his versatility. Turning from the early modern trade policy treated in his dissertation, he now dealt with an entirely different subject: the biography of Israel Jacobson, the layman usually credited with being the founding father of Reform Judaism in Germany. Up to the 1920's, little had been known about Jacob-

Marcus, the Teacher, prior to 1938.

son and his struggle to establish this new approach to Judaism in Germany, so the essay attracted considerable interest when it first appeared in the Central Conference of American Rabbis *Yearbook*. Some decades later it was published in book form, and Marcus still regards it as one of his most important contributions to Jewish literature. To the present day, no one can write a history of Reform Judaism without using Marcus' *Israel Jacobson* as a primary source. At the conclusion of the book, Marcus summarizes the contribution of Jacobson, and his own evaluation of that contribution:

> Now that two centuries have passed since his birth we are in a position to estimate his achievements and his influence on the history of Jewry and of Reform Judaism. Graetz says correctly that the struggle of the age was a struggle between two justified principles — a struggle to preserve Judaism in its own character and an approximation of Judaism to European culture. Jacobson was one of the outstanding fighters for cultural emancipation and adjustment in Europe in the first two decades of the nineteenth century. . . . (p. 125). Jacobson strove earnestly through his compromise religious service to fight the growing indifference to the ancestral faith. He fought belligerently for political emancipation as a just right. He encouraged trade and industry and science among his fellow-Jews. A sound secular education and a proper command of the vernacular were stressed by him, not only for the average individual, but also for the rabbi and teacher. Religious education for women was for him self-understood. He strove for a type of education in Jewish life that was modern, humane, and moral in its effects. He did not accomplish all that he intended, but he pointed the way that would have to be followed. It was a notable contribution of his to Jewish life that he first helped kill the idea that a Jewish synagogue was synonymous with disorder. It was primarily through him that good taste, simplicity, refinement came back into the Jewish service. These are externals

79

to be sure, but they are indispensable in a truly religious life. . . . (pp. 125-26).

Jacobson's most vital mistake was his failure to realize that Judaism could not live only through a broad system of morals, but also needed the sustenance of a strong inner religious sentiment and a deep knowledge of Jewish life and literature (p. 128).

The interesting thing about Marcus' conclusions regarding the ideas and goals of Jacobson is that they reflect much of what Marcus, too, considers basic in the development and the major contributions of Reform Judaism.

His first major work, *The Rise and Destiny of the German Jew*, was published in 1934 by the Union of American Hebrew Congregations. Shortly after Marcus' return from Germany, Barnett Bricker, rabbi of the Euclid Avenue Temple in Cleveland, was visiting the College. The two of them had lunch together, and in the course of the conversation, Barnett said: "Jake, you are just back from Germany. You know Germany and Jewish life there. You ought to write a book about it." Marcus had wanted to write such a book, but still thought of himself as a nobody and was convinced that he did not have the capacity to write a book that would be accepted by scholars and read by the public.

Samuel Sandmel was the man who finally convinced Jake to write the book on Germany. It was four years in the works, and Sam assisted Jake by editing his English style and helping him with the Latin and Greek references. Unfortunately, Marvin Lowenthal's book, *The Jews of Germany*, came out about the same time as Jake's book on the same subject. Lowenthal's publisher was more aggressive in promoting his book, and consequently its sales were better. In time, though, *The Jews of Germany* was read and largely forgotten, while *The Rise and Destiny of the German Jew* was appreciated and remembered. It got good reviews in newspapers like *The London Times*, and ultimately it survived three printings.

Marcus' book became highly controversial. He made the mistake, one he tended to avoid in his future books, of including a prediction in what was otherwise a thoroughly scholarly work. At the end of his chapter on "The Future of German Jewry," Marcus wrote:

> German Jewry has the will to survive. It is exerting every effort possible to human beings to maintain its vitality in the face of overwhelming odds. World Jewry is united as never before, if not as to the methods, certainly as to the urgent necessity of bringing every resource, financial, political, and moral, to the aid of its stricken brethren. The lesson of Jewish history lends us further assurance that, barring wholesale expulsion or massacre, which seem rather remote even under the implacable hatred of the National Socialists, what has been the "Jewish genius for survival" will manifest itself in Germany. To be sure, there are problems and difficulties which, taken separately, seem well nigh insurmountable. But taken in the aggregate, and balanced against the elements of strength, it does not seem that their weight can be sufficient to turn the scales against survival.
>
> However, one cannot hide this fact: a most distinguished Jewish group has been brutally crippled by the National Socialist German Workers' Party (p. 300).

Marcus' prediction that German Jewry would survive as a viable community, despite Hitler's threats to its existence, was couched in cautious terms as he wrote at the beginning of Nazi rule. He was very sensitive, however, to the broad criticism that was later evoked by his sadly optimistic and wrong conclusions. Nevertheless, *The Rise and Destiny of the German Jews* still stands as a highly respected history of German Jewry from emancipation to the advent of Adolf Hitler. And the final paragraph of the book also stands as both an accurate prediction and a continuing challenge for World Jewry:

The Jew gained political and economic freedom only after a long hard struggle. It required almost as much effort to hew out a place for himself in the realm of culture. Such things are the very marrow of Jewish existence. The Jew will never yield in his struggle for freedom. The Jew will never give up the new light of the Western World (p. 321).

Once *The Rise and Destiny of the German Jew* was published and well received by critics and public alike, Jake felt secure enough to move on to another major project. He had long been interested in the medieval period of Jewish history and had, for some time, been collecting source material that documented and illuminated this dark era of the Jews' desperate struggle for survival. For the next four years Marcus concentrated on putting together a good English-language source book for this important epoch in Jewish history; in 1938 *The Jew in the Medieval World* was published by the Union of American Hebrew Congregations. In his preface to this volume, Marcus presented the purposes and the patterns of thought that had guided his selections of the documents and other materials:

> This source book attempts to reflect the life of the medieval Jew as seen through the eyes of contemporaries. The documents and historical narratives given here have been selected with the view of allowing the actors and witnesses of events—that is, the historical facts—to speak for themselves.
>
> The author of this work has not set out with any conscious, apologetic motive. His sole interest is to give, in translation, material which will reflect conditions as they actually were. . . . The difficulties of selection become more obvious when it is realized that there are at least fifteen centuries of medieval Jewish life, that in this work alone sources are translated from over a dozen languages and dialects, and that the lands treated extend

from the Dutch Colony of New Amsterdam (New York) to the borders of China. Accordingly, the principles that have motivated the selections have been those of importance, interest, clarity, and diversification. It has been attempted, within the compass of a fair-sized volume, to omit nothing of prime importance. We are not sure that we have always succeeded.

The preface thus reflects Marcus' meticulous care in the handling of his materials, his concern for the integrity of the book, and his humility in recognizing his own limitations. Despite his modest disclaimers, the book quickly attracted international recognition. It has been required as a source book for this period of history in many of the foremost university history departments in the English-speaking world. It is the oldest Jewish textbook in America in secondary schools, and it has never been out of print. Its editions have been published in turn by the Union of American Hebrew Congregations, Harper & Row, the Jewish Publication Society of America, and the Atheneum Press. In 1989, because of risings costs in the publishing field, it was no longer financially possible to republish a book with such limited annual sales. Michael Meyer, Professor of History at the Hebrew Union College in Cincinnati, concerned that a basic textbook for medieval Jewish studies might go out of print, arranged through the Hebrew Union College Press for a private printer to bring out another edition, and *The Jew in the Medieval World* is now marketed through Behrman House of New York City.

Naturally at the same time that Marcus was planning, developing, and writing *The Jew in the Medieval World* and the works that followed, he continued teaching some fifteen hours a week; he still taught a wide variety of subjects. He remembers having taught every book in the Bible, in the original Hebrew, of course, with the exception of the major prophets and the Psalms. When Rabbi Michael Aaronson, who had lost his sight in World War I, asked Dr.

Marcus to give him a course on Jewish philosophy, the two men read and studied together Husik's book *A History of Medieval Jewish Philosophy.*

Preparation for courses, and the classroom hours themselves, left little time for writing, for Marcus was always a conscientious teacher. Though he resented having to be the jack-of-all-trades on the faculty, he later recognized that this was an important part of his own development. At this time he was still interested in European Jewish history, convinced that there was a future for him in the study of the socio-economic history of Central European Jewry in the early modern period, the sixteenth and seventeenth centuries. However, the articles he wrote showed a wide range of interests. In 1947 the Hebrew Union College Press published his *Communal Sick-Care in the German Ghetto,* an interesting supplement to *The Jew in the Medieval World.* Marcus was very proud of this study which he deemed a real contribution to European Jewish history.

In the meantime, though, there was an important change in Marcus' teaching program. In the summer of 1942, with more chaplains needed to serve the men and women in World War II, the Hebrew Union College accelerated its program with the addition of summer classes for the men going into the junior class. They were thus able to go out to congregations, temporarily replacing rabbis who had volunteered for the military chaplaincy. Dr. Morgenstern asked Marcus to teach a course in American Jewish history that summer. Thus was launched the first required course in American Jewish history. This was, perhaps, one of the most important turning points in his life! He recognized this when he said: "By this time I was veering toward American Jewish history, although I did not realize that I was. I had long realized that America was to be the great center of Jewish life for the future. I had known it years before this." A year later, in 1943, Marcus wrote an "article on 'Jews' for the *Encyclopaedia Britannica.* It dealt with Jewish life in the modern world and contained material relating to Jews in the United States. Reprinted in subsequent issues of the *Britannica*, it was the first attempt at a scientific account of American Jewish history in a standard reference work" (Chyet, in *Early American Jewish History*, hereafter *EAJH* [pp. 16–17]).

By now it was tragically obvious that the Germans were succeeding in destroying European Jewry, especially the great Jewish cultural and intellectual centers in Germany and Poland. The American Jewish community of almost six million men, women, and children was recognized as the largest, wealthiest, freest Jewish community the world has ever known. However, there had been very little research to provide source material for understanding the early beginnings and the creation of the basic economic, political, religious, and social institutions of American Jewry. True, the American Jewish Historical Society had long been a repository for documents that would be valuable resources for future historians. The Society, however, had no on-going campaign to collect these important papers throughout the country. In addition, a few one-volume histories of American Jewry already existed. They, too, suffered from lack of sources and at best were sketchy outlines of almost three hundred years of American Jewish life. Now Marcus recognized that he must take the leadership in filling this tremendous lacuna.

Jacob R. Marcus, Cincinnati, 1950.

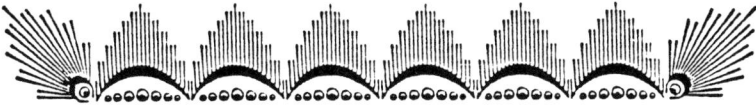

9. MARCUS, THE ARCHIVIST

Jake's interest in American Jewish history dated back to 1916, to that first article for the Wheeling, West Virginia, *Jewish Community Bulletin* on "America: The Spiritual Center of World Jewry." Now his prophecy was being fulfilled, and he would devote the rest of his life to gathering the documents and writing the history of this great Jewish community.

In 1943, Marcus published "A Brief Bibliography of American Jewish History" in the *Jewish Book Annual*, acknowledging the paucity of material available in this field. Shortly thereafter, he suggested to his old friend, Walter E. Rothman, then librarian of the Hebrew Union College, that an American Jewish Archives be developed at the Library. With Rothman's aid, a collection of American Jewish materials was initiated. "In 1946, as chairman of its Committee on Contemporary History and Literature, Marcus recommended to the Central Conference of American Rabbis, convened in Chicago, that congregations undertake to collect and preserve all their records" (Chyet in *EAJH*, p. 17).

Marcus then personally undertook an aggressive campaign to collect congregational minute books, letters, diaries, Jewish newspapers, and other materials that would help paint a portrait of American Jews and the community which they had built. It soon developed that families and congregations were eager to find a repository for these papers. The material began to flow into Cincinnati in increasing volume. Marcus gathered a few students who, working for the College Placement Bureau at fifty cents an hour, microfilmed all of this material to insure that it would never be lost to future historians. Several years after this project began, it became evident that the space in the Hebrew Union College Library was being exhausted, and a suitable building for the rapidly developing Archives would have to be found.

There was a building on the Cincinnati campus, the Bernheim Library, which had been occupied most recently by the National Federation of Temple Brotherhoods but vacated when its board decided to move to New York. One day Marcus walked into the office of Nelson Glueck, newly-appointed president of the College, with a request for the use of the empty Bernheim Library. Marcus told his good friend that this could become the home of the American Jewish Archives, one of the most important contributions that the College could make to the American Jewish community. "Sure, take it," Dr. Glueck said.

The Archives moved into its first home in 1947. There was no budget, of course, and Marcus desperately needed more help than "his boys" could provide. So he went back to the "boss" and asked Dr. Glueck to let him have the services of Dr. Selma Stern Taeubler. Mrs. Taeubler, a highly distinguished historian in her own right, was the wife of one of the German professors the College had rescued from Hitler. The College felt obligated to support her, so it gave her the job as Marcus' first archivist.

The Archives did not have one cent for a budget of its own. Fortunately, a Cincinnati pediatrician, Dr. J. Victor Greenebaum, sat on the Board of Governors of the Hebrew Union College. Something of a gadfly, he liked Marcus and was impressed with the concept of the Archives. When Dr. Greenebaum was made aware that Marcus had no funding for the Archives, he began looking through the College budget at a Board meeting. He found a ten thousand dollar surplus and moved, successfully, that it be given to the Archives. The work could now go forward!

In the next few years, the Archives became the repository for materials gathered from throughout the Americas and Europe. From the beginning it was a unique collection:

minute books of Jewish congregations and of various Jewish societies as well as many personal collections, including the papers, originals or copies, of the colonial merchant-prince Aaron Lopez, and later notables such as Jacob H. Schiff, Louis Marshall, Felix M. Warburg, Julius Rosenwald, and a host of prominent rabbis and Jewish lay leaders. The board records and proceedings of American Jewish institutions since the eighteenth century, as well as many seventeenth century materials, are well represented in the Archives, and many of these documents have been catalogued to facilitate their use by scholars. Indices have been made of various important American Jewish periodicals, including a concordance-type index of Isaac Leeser's mid-nineteenth century publication, *The Occident*.

Marcus' next project was to be the publication of a semi-annual journal which he undertook in 1948, calling it simply *American Jewish Archives*. He patterned it after the *Jewish Quarterly Review*, published in England by Claude Montefiore and Israel Abrahams. Marcus as editor insisted that, like the *Jewish Quarterly Review*, it be written in good, clear English and that its articles be generally on popular themes, not limited to any narrow concept of American Jewish history, but always scientifically defensible. More than forty volumes have already been issued.

The Archives was forty-five years old in 1992. It still occupies the Bernheim Library building, though many of the files of the Archives are now housed next door in the College's administration building. There are seven full-time and two part-time workers on the staff; the total budget runs to about $350,000, much of which is for salaries. The budget of the Archives is incorporated into the budget of the College. Some of the budget comes from interest on endowments which Marcus has encouraged wealthy patrons to contribute. He also raises some 15 percent of his needs through personal solicitations, a portion of which comes from his annual "*schnor* letter" to all the alumni of the College. Marcus is proud of the fact that, according to professional fund-raisers, he does better than most others through his solicitations, for he secures more than four percent of his budget through mail solicitation.

We pause here to share with you some excerpts from Marcus' famous *schnor* (begging) letters. They are striking evidence of why his annual mail solicitation has been twice as successful as the national average for such appeals. These excerpts also give us intimate glimpses into the gentle humor that is characteristic of our professor:

> Puzzled that people should think I am a schnorer, and not knowing what the word meant, I looked it up. It comes from the Middle High German, "to thrum a melody on the musical instrument used by the strolling beggars," or it may come from the Hebrew *"sh'nodar"* —to vow, to make a donation, in order to earn a *mitzvah* [merit in heaven]. As a good Jew, I, of course, much prefer the last explanation. You see, I am out to help you earn mitzvot, and God knows we all need them (1964).

> *   *   *

> Most important of all, 1966 is 19 years since the Archives was founded! Does that constitute a holiday? Of course, for 19 is *begematria, yodteth, Yom Tov* (holiday). Since Y-T also symbolizes *Yezer Tov* (the Good Impulse), we declare this entire 19th year a Yom Tov season in which the Good Impulse is to reign supreme. I call on you to seize the occasion to prepare at least one important American Jewish document for the Archives: an oblong piece of paper, with bank and amount specified, bearing your precious autograph. Oh, how we love such autographs. These are the types of documents which the Archives can accept with the unshakeable conviction that they are authentic and literally true (1966).

> *   *   *

This is my annual schnor letter, although to judge by its contents you might never suspect what I have in mind. In the past, it may be, I've taken unfair advantage by sneaking up on many of you and picking your pockets. Today I won't even plead poverty, for during the past three years our budget has been cut a mere 29 percent. May I say that we are happy more was not taken off. We are resigned, for since the days of Father Abraham we Jews are accustomed to such curtailments of our resources (circumcision) and have learned to get along with what is left (1972).

* * *

The year 1977 marks a very important anniversary. On April 10, 1777 the New York State assembly adopted a constitution that emancipated Jews. It was the first time in Diaspora history that Jews were granted real freedom. The Declaration of Independence was only a Great Promise in 1776, It became something of a reality in 1788 with the adoption of the national constitution giving all Jews equality, at least on the federal level. (All thirteen colonies would not have emancipated their Jews until 1876!) The people of the United States celebrated the adoption of the constitution with a Federal Parade in Philadelphia on July 4, 1788. They saw something then that they had thought would never happen: Rabbi Jacob R. Cohen walking arm in arm with a Catholic priest and a Protestant pastor. The Messiah was just around the corner.

And now that we live in Messianic times what do I ask of you? Plant a rose bush. Buy yourself immortality at bargain prices by sending a check to the American Jewish Archives (1976).

* * *

You have no idea what fun it is to be an American Jewish historian and archivist, all rolled into one. I used to think you met the nicest people only in your dreams; now

I meet them in the documents that come pouring into the Archives. Years ago I met Mrs. Lizzie Black Kander. She was a Milwaukee Jewess who wrote a Jewish cookbook and used the profits to support the local settlement houses; that is why they called it *The Settlement Cookbook*. It is literally true that more Jewesses read her cookbook than the Bible (1977).

*   *   *

The purpose of this letter is to teach you a dirty word: filiopietism, veneration of fellow Jews. Without fear or research the critical mind decries ethnic chauvinism. But, as Dr. Deutsch, my history teacher at the Hebrew Union College, taught me, the fact that a thing may be true is no reason why it is not true. I am daily more and more impressed with our achievements in this country, and whenever I meet a fellow-Jew I am tempted to doff my hat. I fear that I am an academic homosexual. I have fallen in love with my heroes. . . .

As an American Jewish historian the question has often been put to me: What books have helped you? The answer is obvious; my mother's cookbook and your checkbook. I hope I hear from you (1982).

*   *   *

Someone recently asked me, "What are you doing?" I am looking for the truth. Rebecca Franks, a Jewess of eighteenth century Philadelphia, said there is too much truth to have it known. Truth is scarce; it has never been in excess of the demand. Yet I disregard the old lady who said to me: "What is the use of history; let bygones be bygones." I am interested in the millions of American Jews whose experiences often elude recorded history. Hayman Levy, the fur trader, paid John Jacob Astor $1 a day to beat out furs, and Shearith Israel of New York almost beat Levy because he piddled in the synagogue courtyard. Manuel Josephson, the congregational president who wrote the famous letter congratulating George Washington, referred to some of his fellow congregants as sons of b----es! The present chancellor of the City University of New York is Joseph Samson Murphy. His father was an Irish Catholic who worked on a tugboat; his mother was a Polish-born Jewess. Murphy attended a conference on Sholem Aleichem and addressed the audience in Yiddish. Is the Messiah just around the corner? I am always glad to hear from you; let your largess overwhelm me (1984).

* * *

I am busy these days working on a multi-volume history of the Jews in the United States. Sometimes I wonder how smart I am, going into competition with myself. Working frantically to produce a final draft, I am grumpy and irritable. Anything but likeable. Dogs don't come up and pet me. My approach, of course, is critical for I shall strip truth to nakedness. But I hope I will always remain the gentleman; I shall never insult anybody unintentionally. In studying the affluent Reform Jew who is so conspicuous by his absence from the synagogue, I have discovered that in religion nothing fails like success (1985).

* * *

Some of the men and women in the rabbinate write me and ask: How are you Dr. Jake? I answer, I am like King David when he became a senior citizen. I put my clothes to bed and hang myself over the chair. The CCAR [Central Conference of American Rabbis] has provided me with a list of infertility specialists but my guiding light is Joshua Montefiore of Vermont. He was married when he was over seventy and fathered some seven children. You will be interested to hear that women are rushing into the rabbinate. They will work wonders with this apathetic generation, with the assimilated Jew who is the blank page between the Old and New Testament. . . . We expect much from this invasion of the angels. What can we say of them when God deemed Paradise unfinished until a woman smiled among the bowers. . . .

93

I am grateful to all of you for your past gifts to the Archives. Fill the remaining space of this letter with love; it is a fund on which you cannot draw too largely (1988).

* * *

I am now ninety-four years of age; next year I will be ninety-three. My students here at the College will say to me: "But Doctor, we just celebrated your ninety-fourth birthday!" "I know that," I will answer, "but I just figured out that if I keep going on this way, I will have no future. . . ."

P.S. I want you to realize that knowing me is an impoverishing experience. Never forget that the Director of the Archives is a gold-plated panhandler, a human gimme-pig (1980).

One of the important projects that Marcus initiated in the Archives is what he calls "Nearprint." He maintains that the bulk of material of historical significance is ephemera — put out by machines, sent through the mail, and usually winding up in wastebaskets. If this "Nearprint" has any Jewish relevance, it goes into a special section of the Archives. One important section of the Archives deals with the biographies of notable Americans; in all probability thousands of bios are maintained in it for the edification of visiting scholars.

In the spring of 1956, Marcus established the American Jewish Periodical Center for the microfilming of every Jewish periodical published in the United States between 1823 and 1925, and of a selective group after that. The purpose of the Center is to make available to Jewish scholars throughout the world microfilms of Jewish periodical literature on interlibrary loan.

For Marcus, though, the most important fact about the Archives is that men and women thoroughly enjoy coming to pursue research projects there. They are delighted by the helpfulness of the staff who, unlike most archival staffs in

94

the United States and abroad, do not conceive of their function as primarily that of guards, making sure that no one enters their archives without thorough screening and that nothing is taken from their stacks without careful scrutiny. Jews and non-Jews come to work at the Archives from Europe and Israel, from South America and Hong Kong. Under Marcus' guidance, the American Jewish Archives welcomes students and visitors, encourages their interest and their work, and helps them in every way possible. Marcus loves the fact that people continually tell him: "There's no place in the world like this." As he himself says: "No history of American Jewry can be written without recourse to its [the Archives] materials."

The work of the Archives is also enhanced by the presence of graduate Fellows, twelve to eighteen each year, who come to work at the Archives on specific projects for one or two months, and who often share their knowledge with others in the seminars sponsored by the Archives. Marcus always attends these occasions and summarizes the discussion.

In 1958, one year later, a Festschrift, *Essays in American Jewish History*, was produced to celebrate the tenth anniversary of the founding of the American Jewish Archives. In the Foreword to this book, Nelson Glueck wrote:

> The Archives' steady growth, indeed its emergence as a unique institution in American Jewish life, has been due primarily to the gifted direction which it has received from Dr. Jacob Rader Marcus, Adolph S. Ochs Professor of Jewish History. The able leadership which he has supplied has turned the Archives from a bare idea into a living reality . . . within the relatively short space of a decade, the American Jewish Archives has succeeded in assembling over 1,000,000 pages of documentary correspondence, diaries, and congregational minutes, much of it of great historical importance. . . . On this occasion, I am pleased to salute him as a dear and close friend, whose scholarly achievements have brought me personal pride (*EAJH*, pp. xi–xii).

Bertram Korn also wrote in appreciation of his mentor. Korn sought to explain the reasons for Marcus' change of focus in his professional career:

> Even Professor Marcus himself is probably unable to explain just why and exactly when his vision shifted from the more traditional and, in a sense, respected study of the life of the Jews in Europe (and especially in Germany) to the vast, unexplored story of Jewish life on the North American continent. It was probably a combination of several factors: his thorough preparation for history courses at the Hebrew Union College (he has always outlined his lectures for the entire year in advance, and carefully prepared for each session), which made him deeply aware of our comparative ignorance of the Jewish past in our own land; his insight into the millennial movement of Jewish life from center to center, and his comprehension early in the 1930's that, with the growth of Hitlerism, American Jewry must inevitably rise to international pre-eminence in the next period of Jewish history; his own boyhood in the mountains of West Virginia and a native American's love for his own land; and finally his personal involvement (more so than almost any American Jewish scholar) in the day-to-day solution of Jewish problems on the local scene in Cincinnati; in hundreds of other cities and towns where his students serve as rabbis and consult him by telephone and letter when plagued by their own problems, and where he has lectured and taught and learned from his audiences and hosts; and on the national scene where, in the councils of organizations like the American Jewish Historical Society, the B'nai B'rith, the National Jewish Welfare Board, the Union of American Hebrew Congregations, the Jewish Publication Society of America, the National Community Relations Advisory Council, and the Central Conference of American Rabbis . . . to name only a few, he has participated in efforts to mold the Jewish future in America (*EAJH*, pp. xiii–xiv).

In this same year, 1958, Marcus became the president of the American Jewish Historical Society. He recognized that, though the Archives and the American Jewish Historical Society were quite different in their outlook and their approach to their tasks, it was important that there be a good working relationship between the two organizations. He has tried to foster this spirit of cooperation not only with the American Jewish Historical Society, but with regional and local Jewish historical societies as well.

North Suburban Synagogue Beth El

Dr. Jacob Rader Marcus in 1970.

10. MARCUS, THE HISTORIAN

Jacob R. Marcus gave his presidential address at the annual meeting of the American Jewish Historical Society, held in Washington, D.C. at the Library of Congress on February 15, 1958. His subject was: "The Periodization of American Jewish History." In this lecture he divided American Jewish history into four great periods: the Sephardic (1654–1840), the German (1841–1920), the East European (1852–1920) — note the overlapping of the second and third periods — and the American period (1921 and thereafter). Marcus ended the address with a description of the emerging American Jew that is still valid for the present day. He concluded on an optimistic note:

> It is in this age of fusion that there has begun to emerge a *homo novus*, the American Jew. Because of numerous intermarriages and other environmental factors, the "Semitic"-looking Jew — more native to caricature than to reality — has all but vanished. Typical Jewish names have begun to disappear. The American Jew, in appearance, dress, and manners, is indistinguishable from his fellow-citizens. He is an urban white-collar worker who is, at the very least, literate and, indeed, often well-educated; he is liberal in his politics, sympathetic to Judaism and to Jewish education, and imbued with a strong sense of kinship for all Jews. Paradoxical as it may sound, this emerging "American" Jew is more assimilated, culturally, than was his father, yet in many respects as good, if not a better Jew (Reprinted in *Studies in American Jewish History* [SAJH], p. 13).

Marcus' optimism with regard to the future of American Jewry is characteristic of the man. Despite his realistic recognition of the ongoing threat of social and economic discrimination, on the one hand, and an enveloping assimilation, on the other, he has steadfastly maintained that we shall survive as a Jewish community. He has further suggested that "this tight Jewish community will have come into being, not simply because we will have wanted it, but because of compulsive historic forces of kinship and rejection" (*SAJH*, p. 226).

This confidence in American Jewry's future is coupled with the very important question that Marcus raised in his address at the Dropsie College for Hebrew and Cognate Learning in Philadelphia, on June 2, 1955, when that highly respected graduate school of Jewish learning awarded Dr. Marcus an honorary degree. Having stated that we shall survive as a Jewish community, Marcus then asked:

> But why should we survive? Is survival an end in itself? Surely it is not wrong to live, to maintain hallowed and beloved traditions. But I would like to believe that if we retain group identity within a larger context, then that separatism must be inspired by moral considerations. I would like to believe that, if I walk my own way, it is because I have a purpose, because I have something to give.

It is here that we see Jacob Marcus not only as an optimist, but as a man whose optimism is founded on deep religious convictions. He is not religious in the Orthodox sense (though he has chosen never to eat pork products or shell fish in conformity with that aspect of *kashrut*). He has strong convictions, though, that individually and collectively as a Jewish community, there must be a moral imperative in our survival. Marcus concluded his address at Dropsie with this challenge to the religious consciousness of American Jewry:

We have come upon sorry times. The long, liberal century that began in 1789 with the French Revolution died catastrophically at its height in 1919 when the Versailles Peace Treaty was signed. We are in the midst of a world of gathering clouds and impending tragedy. Christianity is on the decline; paganism, brutality, callous hard cruelty are in the ascendant. We are living in a world that seems increasingly indifferent to kindness, to love, to human decencies. It is this situation that rises to challenge the Jew to survive purposefully, to justify his separatism.

Let us survive to the end that we shall survive to create a universal society where men are tolerant of one another, where nationalism is not the highest good, and where world peace is not a hollow mockery, but a sacred and a cherished ideal.

Surely the time has come for a new categorical imperative to teach nations to act toward one another according to the same spiritual standard that determines the relations of one moral individual to another. Is this not after all the sum total of all prophetic teaching? Is this not why we call ourselves Jews? If it is not to preserve these great truths, then why have we writhed in agony in the fiery crucible for over two thousand years?

The only salvation for all of us lies in a moral society. Let us work toward that end. When all is said and done: "The fear of God is the beginning of wisdom" (*SAJH*, pp. 229-30).

In 1951, just four years after Jacob Marcus created the American Jewish Archives, his first major volume of American Jewish history was published by the Jewish Publication Society of America. It is worth noting that this book, *Early American Jewry*, Volume I, which was the first in-depth study of the mostly pre-Revolutionary history of the Jews of New York, New England, and Canada, appeared just three years before the American Jewish community was to celebrate its tercentenary.

To understand the tremendous challenge that Marcus faced in this pioneering work, we have only to read, in the preface to this volume, his answer to three vital questions; the first was "How is it possible to write American Jewish history?" Marcus' response:

> . . . it is no more difficult today to write American Jew-
> ish history than it is to make bricks without clay. The
> clay, the sources, are still to be dug up. In this field
> there are no biographical or historical dictionaries,
> no atlases, no auxiliary works, few collected sources, no
> satisfactory union list of Jewish serials, no genealogical
> tables, not a single complete history of the American
> Jew that satisfies the canons of modern methodology
> and criticism. The basic tools with which every his-
> torian works are still missing (*Early American Jewry*
> [*EAJ*], I:vii).

Marcus recognized that it was he alone who was now under-taking the responsibility to create these tools, aids, and reference works.

Another important question that Marcus had to address before writing the history of the American Jew was how to define a Jew. No single definition was satisfactory either to Jews or non-Jews, and Marcus realized that any such defi-nition would be subjective. His definition, later to be the same one accepted by David Ben-Gurion when he was Prime Minister of Israel, was simply: "Anyone was a Jew who said he was a Jew" (*EAJ*, I:viii).

Finally, in preparation for his pioneer work, Marcus ad-dressed the question of what is American Jewish history. His answer is most important, because it laid the foundation upon which his research and his publications would be based. His response to his own question was:

> In a more restricted sense it is the history of the Jewish
> religious community. In the broadest sense it is also the

study of the individual Jew — or of Jewry — in relation to the larger community. Thus American Jewish history may also embrace inquiry into civil and political rights, economic patterns, cultural standards and accomplishments, social acceptance and social goals. . . .

The study of American Jewry invites the inquiring mind. It is an integral part of the larger field of American history. It is a particular which brightly illumines the general history, especially in the crucial early and formative years of America (*EAJ*, I:viii–ix).

Most important of all, though, is Marcus' concept of his role as an American Jewish historian. It is typical of his response to every facet of life, his relationships with colleagues and with students, his genuine interest in people of every walk of life, and his ability to empathize with them. He interprets history in its broadest sense, because he is not a student of facts alone, but of human beings and their impact on the society which they are helping to mold. Here is how Marcus understands his role as the first scientific American Jewish historian:

The prime purpose of the writer of this work was better to understand the American Jews of the colonial and the early national period. From the vantage point of centuries he wanted to catch them unawares and to peer into their souls — at least to peep over their shoulders as they wrote to one another.

Like many others today, he has found little human satisfaction in much of the historical data as usually presented. Not that the conventional method of selection is inadequate. Quite correctly the historian of today emphasizes ideas, movements, and trends. But in this effort the average individual disappears. The part is swallowed up in the whole. We seek, as a counterbalance, to snatch the individual from the anonymous mass and to delineate his role in the larger events. We want to humanize our knowledge, to understand the average

Jew, the small shopkeeper, if you will, in his everyday life. Once we begin to describe his actions in some detail, he begins to take on flesh and blood. He comes to life. The medium we have used to accomplish our purpose is the personal letter. This study of the early American Jew is built around the letters and petitions he wrote.

In this presentation we have sought to touch at least on basic movements. If we have succeeded at all in this effort, then this work is an informal history of the early American Jew. It does not hew to the line mechanically, stubbornly, like the surveyor who cuts straight through to his distant goal. It is more like a broad river moving leisurely from source to mouth, winding through broad valleys, covering great stretches of territory. By travelling on a meandering stream, one moves much more slowly—but one learns to know the countryside (*EAJ*, I:xiii–xvii).

The second volume of *Early American Jewry* appeared two years later, in 1953. It focuses on the Jews of Pennsylvania and of the colonies and states further south. Of particular interest are the concluding 150 pages which are a survey of the entire period, 1655–1790, of American Jewish life. It describes who the immigrants to this new world were and why they came; how they adjusted economically and how they lived as Jews in their communities. It examines their culture, as they began to emerge as distinctly new characters in the panorama of Jewish history: the American Jew.

Marcus summarizes his characterization of the new American Jew in the final chapter of Volume II of *Early American Jewry*. He wrote:

One is almost tempted to say that the Jew of the Revolution and of the post-Revolutionary generation was a changed man. The common political and military struggle after 1775, the common suffering, unleashed something in his psyche. Before the war his prime interest was his livelihood. To be sure, the economic avenue was the

104

only road then open to him. Another, the political, was closed to him because of his religion. He preferred obscurity; he had little to say. But with the Revolution the wellsprings of hope within him gushed forth and with it the desire, the intention, to fight for personal and communal recognition, for freedom and for equality. This man was different, or reborn; he was insistent on his rights, proud, firm in his resolution to receive his political due. He was a new man (II:547) . . . he [was] a city dweller, a member of the middle class, literate but not literary.

He [was] a merchant, skilled, enterprising, venturesome in commerce and shipping, a man of courage. Good common sense and a willingness to work hard were among his chief traits. He was an individualist, more vigorous in asserting himself than the typical Jew in a well-regulated, urban, European Jewish community. There could be no question of his loyalty to his faith, but, like his Christian neighbors, he was not submissive to religious authority, such as it was.

This man looked just like his neighbors; his features were not particularly "Jewish"; he had the suspicion of a foreign brogue, but he was obviously a person who had sloughed off the externals of Europe. His culture was English. Conversation with him would disclose that politically he was an egalitarian, a republican. As one who had lived for years among Gentiles, this Jew numbered among them intimate friends whom he admired and trusted. He was willing, when he could, to join them in common philanthropy. Like Rivera and Lopez, who had been close to President Stiles of Yale, he was happy to do anything that could be "honorable" to the Jewish "nation." Good relations with a neighbor, with the wider community, were important. Sign a petition to reopen the theatre? Of course! Politics? An office? Why not? If he needed anything to help him make up his mind, he had only to look about him to see everyday men whom he knew occupying the highest offices, sitting in the cabinet with the President himself. I'm just as good

as the next man, was his unspoken thought. This fellow
believed in himself; he had complete confidence in his
future in this land (II:552–53).

These reflections of the author, of what the "composite"
American Jew of the seventeenth and eighteenth centuries was
like, tell us a great deal about the author himself. The son
of immigrant parents, Marcus was very sensitive to the importance of Jews becoming well integrated into the political
and social life of their new homeland. He knew the struggles
of immigrant families, but he also knew first hand of their
successes, if they but persevered. Marcus believed that this
great democracy would be a haven for Jews, and that the
early Jewish settlers had done much to undergird the position
of the Jew as a first-class citizen in this exciting new world.
Marcus' love for America, and his faith in the future of the
Jew in this land, are reflected throughout these two volumes.
Though there is always the danger of oversimplification in
generalizing about the characteristics and the personality of
a community, Marcus draws on individual letters and diaries
to make these volumes a very personal history, and he does
it quite well.

Early American Jewry was widely acclaimed by scholars
and reviewers. Among the quotations from reviews of Volume I which appeared on the back of the dust jacket of
Volume II, was a statement by Moshe Davis in the *American
Historical Review*. Dr. Davis wrote: "Dr. Marcus brings skill,
painstaking research and scientific method to his work. For
this alone, *Early American Jewry* is an estimable contribution
to the expanding field of American Jewish historiography."
And the reviewer in the *Mizrachi Outlook* said: "The two
parts of this history may well become the definitive study of
our ancestors on this continent."

Two years after the appearance of the second volume
of *Early American Jewry*, The Jewish Publication Society of
America published Marcus' three volumes of *Memoirs of*

American Jews, 1775-1865. This collection of biographical vignettes, letters, and personal recollections of representative American Jews was prepared in commemoration of the three hundredth anniversary of American Judaism. When Marcus was asked by a critic what was "Jewish" about these reminiscences, he replied:

> They *are* part of the Jewish experience in this land. The division between general history and the history of the Jew in America is frequently arbitrary and artificial. Every aspect of Jewish life here is part of American life. . . . These volumes of autobiographical narratives describe in detail the realities of immigration, of business life, of emerging Jewish communities, of a changing Judaism, of the subtle process of acculturation and integration. These happenings are the essence of nineteenth-century American history — and they are the heart of the Jewish experience. American Jewish history is the story of *all* that happened to the Jew as an American (*Memoirs of American Jews*, I:5).

To this definition of American Jewish history, Marcus added a very significant parenthetical statement. He noted that since one motivation for creating an American Jewish history might be filiopietism, the decisions as to what would or would not be included "will not be uninfluenced by apologetics." Marcus was an honest historian who knew that no scholar could be completely objective.

Dr. Marcus was also very frank when asked for his philosophy of American Jewish history. He replied:

> I have no specific philosophy of American Jewish history. As in general Jewish history, I believe that the Jew is closely integrated with his background. This is particularly true in America where the Jews have never been a distant political group, but always part of the American body politic. I am very much interested in the religious, social, economic, and cultural life of the Jew

here. I believe that he is a cultural entity, has always been one, and will always remain one. . . . The American Jew is not completely subject to his general American background. His history may be, to a certain extent, independent of that background, although that background must always be very closely studied (Chyet in *SAJH*, p. 21).

In his introduction to the *Memoirs*, Marcus explained further that the difficulty with trying to develop a philosophy that would encompass all or most American Jews was the fact that they came from at least a half-dozen European countries and had scattered throughout the United States. They also ranged from cultured men and women to those with very limited education. He then draws a most interesting conclusion as to marked regional differences within the American Jewish community:

Without doubt one of the significant conclusions to be drawn from this material is that the Southern Jew was the most cultured Jew in the ante-bellum period. The acculturation pattern that he developed was to be followed a generation later in other parts of the United States. . . .

As far as the native American Jew was concerned, there were — to use my own terminology — probably two types: the Southern, and the National-American. . . . The National-American includes the Northerner and the Westerner, who ranged from the Alleghenies to the Pacific Coast. He, too, was a type, but because of our lack of perspective, we find it difficult to envisage him, for he is the source of our common national type of today. He is the present-day American. The core of the differences between the Southerner and the National-American lies in their attitudes toward free and slave labor, and in the conflicts between the dominant plantation economy of the South and the farm and urban economy of the North (*Memoirs of American Jews*, I:25).

Both volumes of *Early American Jewry* and the three volumes of the *Memoirs* had been dedicated to Nettie. The dedication in the former set was particularly touching:

> Many years ago a graduate student at the University of Berlin dedicated his thesis:
>
> To
> Pretty Nettie Brody
>
> Today, after twenty-five years of married life, he dedicates this book to the same woman.

Tragically, Nettie died in July, 1953, after the *Memoirs* had been completed, but before they were published. Though Marcus continued to teach at the College and to supervise the work at the Archives, he found it difficult to settle down to his rigorous writing schedule. Finally, in 1959, the Hebrew Union College Press published Marcus' *American Jewry, Documents, Eighteenth Century*. This volume was dedicated to a Cincinnati Jewish widow whom Jake and Nettie had known for many years and who was to be his friend until her own death. She helped him become part of the social life of the Jewish community once again.

American Jewry, Documents, Eighteenth Century is not a continuous narrative like *Early American Jewry*. Rather it is a collection, for the most part, of hitherto unpublished manuscripts dealing with eighteenth century North American Jews. Marcus divided the material into four parts: The Personal Life, The Religious Life, The General Community, and Commerce and Trade. He also provided introductions to the material, placing the letters, documents, minute books, newspaper accounts and advertisements, in their proper perspective. In his preface to the book, Marcus says: "This is one of the few reference books that portrays the actual day-to-day living of the urban businessman in early America. In this respect, I believe, this work is unique" (viii). The volume has proven to be invaluable for those for whom

Marcus primarily gathered the material and provided appropriate introductions: the amateur historian, the beginning student, and the nonprofessional reader, as well as scholars and writers in the field of American Jewish history.

Six years later, in 1965, the Society of Jewish Bibliophiles published a small volume of documents Marcus had collected under the title of *On Love, Marriage, Children, and Death, Too*. This collection reflected another aspect of Marcus' life about which he felt deeply, but which he rarely discussed, his own family life, beset as it was by so many tragedies.

> Life and history, one is often tempted to say, begin with death. Facing the inevitability of the end, a responsible husband and father makes provision for his family in his will. Then, when he passes away, a new generation steps forward for a fleeting moment to carry on the long, many-linked chain of tradition. Historians, however, in their dogged pursuit of the facts of death and life and accomplishment, only too often forget the forces driving a man to do what he does. Among these forces there are none greater than love: the love a man has for his wife, his children, his mother (p. 1).

The next major work that Marcus produced, in 1969, was his *Studies in American Jewish History*. This volume contains a collection of essays written over the years, essays in which he seeks to define and trace the developing patterns in the American Jewish community. As significant as is the content of these essays, equally important is the scientific approach with which he laid the foundations for scholarship in this new field of study. The inside cover of the book jacket sums this up admirably:

> The essays are characterized by a faithful adherence to the facts, a critical evaluation of the data, and a complete avoidance of apologetics. Dr. Marcus' methodological studies are basic in any scholarly approach to the relatively new discipline of American Jewish history.

Marcus established the role of the synagogue as the first important unifying factor in American Jewish life. From 1654 to 1776, he maintained, it was the synagogue that the immigrants and their children clung to as their means of survival in this strange new land. His own predilection for the importance of the religious aspect of Jewish life is seen in his statement that the history of colonial Jewry could be written around Shearith Israel of New York, which he characterizes as the mother synagogue on this continent (p. 16).

Though the synagogue could serve as the unifying factor for the small Sephardic communities that were the core of the first period in American Jewish life, it could not perform the function on a nation-wide basis for the German immigrants who spread out in America even as the country itself spread west. However, for them, too, the synagogue would remain what Marcus called "the spinal column of American Jewry." He noted, though, that an increasing number of Jews were more interested in surviving as a social group than in surviving through religion alone. As the Jews of Central Europe began to come to this country in greater numbers and migrated southward and westward, there was a growing sense of need for the German Jewish "tradition of a federated Jewish community," plus a strong feeling of kinship, that fired the urge for unity. Marcus maintained that "this urge to unity, to establish agencies that will hold them together by implementing their religious and social aspirations, is the theme of American Jewish history from 1840 to the present day" (pp. 16-17). In the twentieth century "this many-faceted approach to the cultural and social assimilation of the East European Jews and their children into the older American Jewish community" continued. Once more it was "the unification of all Jews, natives and immigrants, through the accomodation of the Jew and of his religion to American life and culture," that would be the dominant theme in American Jewish life (p. 19).

Marcus saw that this need for unity was also fired by a

general sense of insecurity, brought about in large measure by the consciousness of an emergent anti-Semitism spreading from France and Germany in the 1880's to penetrate American life. Marcus pointed out that this made for an apologetic tendency in American Jewish historical research and writing when these were first undertaken in the 1890's. This was a pattern that Marcus earnestly sought to correct in his own approach to American Jewish history. He was a pioneer in recognizing that by the 1940's the American Jewish community was the largest (five million) and most opulent the world had ever seen, and therefore had to take a serious and realistic look at its origins. To this end he pioneered the scientific discipline of American Jewish history.

As an historian, Marcus also brought the lessons of the past to bear upon the current situation in which the American Jews found themselves. In his excellent essay on "Background for the History of the American Jew," he wrote:

> History is not without some logic. People create the institutions they need in order to survive. That explains the development of local Diaspora Jewish communities ever since the Jews were exiled to Babylonia in the sixth pre-Christian century. But the local Jewish community, whether in present-day America or in ancient Babylonia, is not an island. It cannot live Jewishly by and for itself alone. To effectuate its purposes, to defend itself, and to move forward, it requires the spiritual, cultural, intellectual, and political support of a supra-local, or national Jewish community (p. 211).

From this historical perspective, Marcus became, in the 1940's, one of the leading voices urging American Jewry to achieve its long-sought-for unity through establishment of a national organization that would coordinate and give direction to the work of already existing local and national bodies. He saw that the Holocaust had forced American Jewry to emerge from being "little more than a spiritual colony of Europe" to becoming the true heir to the mantle of World Jewish leadership. It was, he pointed out, the only sizable Jewish community in the world still free and still surviving. As Marcus put it:

> *Noblesse oblige*, has now been added to all the other reasons driving American Jewry to organize on a local, regional, and — above all — national level. For now, not only is such an organization essential if the community is to function smoothly . . . but it is no less essential if the community is to fulfill the ineluctable obligation that history has imposed on it: to help all Jews everywhere in the world (p. 212).

The first such recognition of American Jewry's responsibility for the fate and future of fellow-Jews throughout the world, Marcus pointed out, had come in 1859 in response to the Edgar Mortara case. An Italian-Jewish child had been abducted by the Catholic authorities in Bologna. Marcus reported that

> The plight of a Jewish mother, bereaved of her son, shocked even Catholic monarchs. The Jews of the French Empire were sufficiently agitated to create the Alliance Israelite Universelle, while the indignant members of America's miniscule Jewish community — numbering about 100,000 — organized themselves into the Board of Delegates of American Israelites. Primarily a civic defense and overseas relief agency, the Board was never able to establish its authority and in 1878 was absorbed by the younger, more powerful Union of American Hebrew Congregations as the Union's Board of Delegates on Civil and Religious Rights (pp. 212-13).

Unfortunately, though, neither the Union nor B'nai B'rith had succeeded in becoming the national organization capable of representing and speaking for American Jewry. Marcus noted that these failures led ultimately to the formation in 1906 of the American Jewish Committee, but Marcus pointed out that its "highly paternalistic leadership" (p. 213) prevented it, too, from ever becoming the national organization representing all American Jews.

Marcus' vision of a strong national coordinating and advisory body for American Jewry was augmented by his equally firm conviction that an over-all Jewish international agency was also imperative to defend Jews around the world and to protect the State of Israel against those political enemies determined to destroy it. The creation of such a world Jewish body, he has felt, would be dependent primarily on the leadership of American Jews.

Who is this American Jew whom Marcus envisaged, some twenty-five years ago, as being prepared to assume the mantle of leadership for World Jewry? At the end of his essay on "The Background for the History of the American Jew," Dr. Marcus adds to his description of this new Jew:

> . . . because he knows more, he is more sympathetic; with knowledge have come loyalty and devotion, not in parochial but in broad universal terms, to the ideals of his people and to the welfare of even the most distant Jewries. This growing sense of kinship and the "style" of American life in general will bring the majority of Jews back into the synagogue. Some will come only to associate with their fellows. Others will seek education for their children and themselves. Some will remain to pray, and in a world where science reaches out to embrace the infinite, they will reverently identify themselves once again with the spiritual ideals of their fathers.
>
> What is actually in process in this generation, on the eve of a new century, is a blending of Americanism and Judaism. Like the historic mergers of Hellenism and Judaism, Arabic and Jewish culture, German methodology and Jewish lore, the new American Jewish synthesis will be expressed in the vernacular; like Plato's Greek commentaries, or Maimonides' Arabic *Guide*, or

Zunz's German monographs, it will take a literary form. It will constitute, in effect, a fusion between the Jewish intellectual heritage and the various currents of thought prevalent in contemporary and future America. When, ultimately, books of enduring value begin to appear, works embodying the best in both cultures, books of such lasting worth that they will merit translation into other languages, including Hebrew, then we shall have witnessed the birth of another Golden Age in Jewish life. Barring a "historical accident," such a development is inevitable on this soil (pp. 220–221).

Marcus' prophecy has proven to be remarkably accurate in many respects, though his expectation that the majority of American Jews would find their way back into the synagogue has not been confirmed.

His picture of the new American Jew, and the community in which this Jew will live, can best be described by a paragraph that he wrote in his essay on "The Future of American Jewry" in this same collection of *Studies in American Jewish History:*

This tight Jewish community will have come into being, not simply because we will have wanted it, but because of compulsive historic forces of kinship and rejection. This community, this commonality, will come because it is already here. We can suffer it because as objects of history we have no choice, or else we can bend it to our purposes and become the subjects of history. I suggest that we make history(!) (p. 226).

The next major work that Marcus undertook was his three-volume study of *The Colonial American Jew, 1492–1776,* published in 1970. These volumes were a sequel to *Early American Jewry,* following the same basic pattern of interpreting significant documents of the period. This primary source material allows past generations to speak for themselves in presenting the economic, political, and social history of the American Jew.

In his preface to Volume I, Marcus answers the question that many of his contemporaries asked: Why was he devoting his life to the study of American Jewish history? Did this history have any lasting significance? His answer is very much to the point:

> The basic premise, the essential *fact* to which I am committed in my work, is that the Jews constitute a "people." Since their earliest days on these shores, they have been an organized group, united by common institutions, traditions, beliefs, an inspiring past, and an unusually strong sense of kinship. Wherever possible, they have tended to live in close proximity to one another. As a tightly-knit fellowship, they have shared common experiences, and the totality of these makes up American Jewish history (*Colonial American Jew*, I:xxiii).
>
> * * *
>
> More to the point, it may be, the Jew is the barometer of history. We have no better way to gauge early America's progress toward social acceptance of new or "peculiar" settlers, toward religious toleration, toward economic and political equality for her citizens, than to study the treatment of the Jew in colonial times. In a profound sense, the Jew of British North America could have said to his Christian neighbors and to the Christian power structure: "What you do unto me, you do unto yourselves" (I:xxiv).

It is obvious that Marcus, the historian, carried on a real romance with colonial Jewry. He respected the resourcefulness and the diligence of these eighteenth-century Jews in sinking deep and firm roots in the rich, fertile soil of America. This admiration and pride in the contribution of colonial Jewry is beautifully expressed in Marcus' summary at the end of Volume III:

What did this man [the colonial Jew] achieve for himself? He moved Europe across the Atlantic, no mean
achievement. Synagogues, schools, charities, a "community" were transferred here, nailed down and fas-
tened, firm and viable and visible enough to attract
hundreds of thousands of others who would never have
come to a "waste howling wilderness" where there were
no Jewish institutions. A dozen families in seventeenth-
century New York laid the foundations for a twentieth
century community of nearly six million Jews. Colonial
Jewry wrote the pattern of acculturation which made it
possible for the Jew to remain a Jew and to become an
American. The pioneers of the eighteenth century succeeded in making an exemplary transition from a still
medieval European Jewish life to the new American
world of modernism and personal freedom
    What did this man achieve for the land? Not that
this Jew was conscious of it, but together with all dis-
senters—and every American denomination suffered
disabilities in one or another of the provinces—he
helped teach his neighbor religious tolerance. The fruit
of this tolerance was respect for the personality of the
individual. The pre-revolutionary Jew made no contribution to the literature of the colonies; he cleared no
forests and ploughed no furrows—yet he too built the
land. He, as much as any other, made American life
more comfortable through the necessities and the luxur-
ies he provided. It is true that the trader needed his cus-
tomers, but it is equally true that neither city craftsmen
nor toiling rustics could exist without him. It is true, too,
that in a literal numerical sense the Jew was one man in
a thousand, but in an economy where an overwhelming
majority of all who labored made their living on the soil,
it is difficult to overstress the importance of the shopkeeper and the merchant (II:1341-42).

Marcus' research into the files of American Jewish history
took him into many fascinating area. One of the areas was
delineating the role of the American Jewish woman in her

people's history. This led, in 1981, to the publication of his two volumes entitled *The American Jewish Woman*. The second volume contained a large collection of documents that emphasized the contribution of American Jewish women to their country and to the Jewish community of America. The first volume is a highly readable narrative, based in large part on the documents published in the second volume.

In the preface to the narrative history, Marcus begins by asking "why did I write this book?" He answers his own question:

> Actually I was pressured into it by colleagues and associates, and now that this monograph is completed I am grateful to them. The Jewish woman has been ignored in the standard chronicles of this country's Jewry. There are exceptions, of course, but the few women included can be counted on the fingers of one hand. There can be no question: there is an American Jewish woman's history that goes back to September 1654. All American Jewish annalistic works deal with men, a numerical minority among the Jews; there has been no full-length, scientifically conceived, source-based book detailing the lives and adventures of American Jewesses. They were, and still are, a majority of all Jews in this land (p. xi).

Marcus also made certain in the preface that no one would construe this work as "another feminist liberation narrative. . . . It is obvious that such a book will not only record her activities but also her 'disabilities' under which she has labored for at least three thousand years in a patriarchal religious society" (p. xii).

Professor Marcus recognized that in this work, as in so many earlier volumes, he was the pioneer, doing the spade-work for generations of Jewish historians yet to come. He relished this role; he was proud of the fact that he was not only bequeathing to future scholars in his field a wealth of material to serve as the foundation for their research, but demonstrating the scientific techniques that would give greater validity to their work. He wrote:

> Ten years from today, another history of the American Jewish woman will have to be written . . . I hope. A new school of Jewish historians is now rising; many of them are women; they will do justice to their sex. Books on the Jewish woman will appear; they must be written. They, the writers of tomorrow, will produce a monographic literature that is not in existence today. I deem it a privilege, with the limited resources at hand, to present a history that will serve — if for nothing else — as a point of departure. The periodization, I believe, is grounded on solid data. One may well cherish the hope that future writers of American Jewish history will give American Jewesses their due as sentient human beings, as women, as Jews (p. xii).

It is obvious here, as throughout the two volumes, that Marcus sought to give Jewish women their rightful place in American Jewish history. Moreover, he was keenly sensitive to the injustices that had been done to women throughout Jewish history, and consequently he sought to reclaim for them their rightful place.

All of the aforementioned books by Jacob R. Marcus were, in a sense, a prelude to his magnum opus which was yet to come. He had begun planning, in the 1940's, to write a one-volume "definitive" history of the American Jew. Though several attempts had been made by other authors, none satisfied what Marcus felt was sadly needed. It was imperative, he felt, to write a succinct, thoroughly scientific source-based history of the American Jew. There was no such work. Within a short time, though, Marcus realized that he had set for himself an impossible task. With all the material now available in the American Jewish Archives and other sources, it seemed impossible to do justice to over three hundred years of American Jewish history in a single volume. He adjusted his sights and began systematically planning not for one but for four volumes. Even with this enlargement of conception, the goal was a formidable one, but the professor was dogged in his determination to produce these volumes. Immediately following the publication of *The American Jewish Woman*, he began in earnest the final preparations for the writing of his history of U.S. Jewry. By the late eighties the books were virtually complete.

Then came the task of finding a publisher for the four volumes. Up to this point in Marcus' career this had never been a problem. His first two books, *The Rise and Destiny of the German Jew*, and *The Jew in the Medieval World*, had established his reputation as a scholar and author. His subsequent writings in American Jewish history and his reputation as the outstanding teacher and lecturer in his field made many publishers eager to produce his books. Times had changed, however. The cost of paper and of printing had risen astronomically, and publishers were wary of committing themselves to four volumes that would have limited sales. Two years passed before Wayne State University Press finally agreed to become the publisher. The plan was to bring out a volume a year for the next four years. The first volume appeared in 1989, followed by a second about a year and a half later. The third volume was published in 1993. The final volume should appear in 1994.

Scholars and literary critics have been lavish in their praise of the first two volumes. They have lauded the scientific methodology, the exhaustive research, and the readability of both volumes. Undoubtedly these volumes, and volumes three and four, together with the three volumes on colonial Jewry, will be the classic reference works in American Jewish history for generations to come. The four-volume *United States Jewry, 1766–1985*, is the crowning glory of Marcus' career. This is not to say that more books will not continue to come from his pen; he still writes each legal-size page literally with pen in hand. As long as his strength holds out, God willing, to a hundred and twenty, Marcus will be at his desk six mornings a week, fifty-two weeks a year, producing additional books that will illuminate the annals of American Jewish life. None, however, past or future, will ever equal the magnificent contribution to American and World Jewry that the four-volume *United States Jewry* represents.

Dr. Jacob Rader Marcus today.

11. THE BROADER OUTREACH

Marcus' primary commitment has been to the Hebrew Union College, which educated and ordained him and gave him his first and only teaching position, and to the American Jewish Archives that he founded and developed into what is probably the greatest repository of American Jewish source data. However, he recognizes the importance of other organizations to which he has committed both time and talent. Foremost among these have been the Jewish Publication Society of America, the Central Conference of American Rabbis, and the various organizations that nurture and support the State of Israel.

For many years Marcus served as chairman of the important and prestigious Publications Committee of the Jewish Publication Society of America. At the Society's annual meeting in 1941, he gave an address that was emotionally charged and challenging. He began by stating:

> It would be no violation of the surface truth to say that the Jewish Publication Society of America is unquestionably the greatest institution of its kind that modern Jewry has created. But utterances of this sort involve a subtle danger, for they assume a state of final and definitive accomplishment which might be taken as an appropriate signal for relaxation into an attitude of smug and unproductive complacency. These are times, when every present moment is a battleground on which opposing forces are struggling to gain possession of the future. In such times, to evaluate ourselves and our institutions in terms of past accomplishment alone is to fall into a fatal error from which there can be no recovery. The

merits of the past no longer constitute by themselves a reliable index of true greatness. That alone is great which bears within itself the seeds of mighty achievement in the days to come. Greatness, then, is not an accomplished fact; it is a noble promise ("New Literary Responsibilities," *American Jewish Year Book [AJYB]* 43:784).

Marcus proceeded to give a brief history of the Society and of the individuals who led it through difficult years of birth and rebirth. He then dramatically rehearsed the fate of the Jewish presses and cultural institutions in Europe since the advent of Hitler. Marcus reminded his audience that the Soncino Press and many of its invaluable plates had been destroyed in the bombing of London. The Society for Jewish Studies in France no longer existed. The great Jewish cultural center of Poland was no more. The German Jewry that had been the inspiration for World Jewry's cultural and academic life had been destroyed completely. All of this made the responsibilities of the Jewish Publication Society most awesome:

The Jewish Publication Society is the only surviving literary medium of mass instruction west of Jerusalem. Five million Jews on this continent must find much of their inspiration through us. And lest the magnitude of this task escape us, it should be pointed out that we are not merely five million. At this moment we are Jewry — the only Jewry free to act. We are the whole army: the vanguard, the main body, and the rear guard. We are the heart of a Jewish life which must be maintained and whose spirit must be strengthened ever anew. This is the hour of our crisis. And the crisis is a double one.

The burden is solely ours to carry: Jewish culture and civilization and leadership are shifting rapidly to these shores. Men will need books, books in the vernacular — we must supply them. Here on these shores, the scholars we have bred and the scholars we have sheltered will write new books, steeped in the wisdom and lore that

124

have flourished in Europe since that day a thousand years ago when the Babylonian luminaries first brought the torch of learning to the Mediterranean lands. These books we will publish. This is our privilege, our sacred obligation, and our magnificent opportunity (*AJYB*, 43:489-90).

Marcus also used this occasion to sound a solemn warning regarding the plan and the purpose of Germany. This was the year 1941, when most Americans and even a considerable number of American Jews did not yet take Adolf Hitler seriously and thought the reports of atrocities in the concentration camps were gross exaggerations. With the fervor of the prophets, Marcus declared:

> At this moment there is flourishing in Germany a National Socialist Empire that is determined to rule Europe and the world. This powerful state seeks to gain friends in every land by preaching a gospel of hate. It moves calmly and deliberately, but beneath the quiet surface of its activity there is couched an implacable malice that is burning at white heat. We know that. Anti-Semitism is to be the wedge that will clear the way for the philosophy of despotism. It is to be the tie that will bind all free nations of the world together in a bond of common sympathy with this new Hitlerian Reich. In Germany's international crusade for anti-Semitism the Jew is denounced as the curse of modern civilization, damned as the source of liberalism and democracy, and anathematized as the cause of all social misery and human misfortune. It is affirmed therefore that the destruction of the Jew and of democracy are the only hopes for this war-ridden world. The Reich is bending all of its energies to convince the world that it is the beneficent mission of Germany to assume European hegemony, to prove to the nations that the destruction of the Jew in present-day Europe is a necessary step in the furtherance of civilization (*AJYB*, 43:790).

There is but one effective answer to lies and half-truths—and that is the whole truth. It is our task to publish books, both popular and technical, the scientific integrity of which is beyond the shadow of suspicion. Objective scholars possess the criteria to determine with whom lies the truth. Every volume that comes forth from Munich must be countered by a volume from the City of Brother Love [Philadelphia, where the Jewish Publication Society was, and is, headquartered]. This is a new and added responsibility, a grave responsibility that requires vision and courage and unyielding tenacity. . . . I have said that ours is a grave responsibility; it is also a great opportunity. I believe we shall be worthy of it (*AJYB*, 43:791).

Eight years later, in 1949, Marcus spoke to the Society again as it celebrated its sixtieth anniversary. After a fascinating anecdotal history of the Society, Marcus concluded his speech with this salient observation:

In 1888 there was established in this country a very interesting type of publication society. It was called the Minerva Publication Company. It was the most vicious anti-Semitic organization and publication institution of its type that had yet been developed in this country, and it was in that same year that the Jews of this country thought it was advisable to establish some form of cultural instrumentality that would fight assimilation, and that would encourage Jews to be loyal to the finest traditions of their faith.

And so in 1888 we created the Jewish Publication Society of America. One of the very first books that it published was a history, it was *Outline of Jewish History*. I think that the publication of that book was symbolic because by publishing a history of the Jews we proclaimed to the world that we wanted to declare our kinship with all Jews everywhere, that we were at one with them, and that we wanted to maintain our loyalty to all that was fine in our past.

126

Since that time we have grown, the Society has grown with America. When we began in 1888 we did not have a single book to our credit. Today we have published over 240 different titles and over 4,500,000 copies. In 1888 this was a small group of Jews. Today we have over 5,000,000. This is the largest Jewish community in the world today. Our society has grown with America and has become a great society. Not because our presses have been pounding [out] and have been turning out hundreds of books, hundreds of thousands and millions of words. We believe that we have become a great society because we have published books that make for character, for integrity, and to further culture. We believe that we are a great organization because we make for finer Jews, for finer individuals, for finer American citizens (*Jewish Exponent*, Philadelphia, April 22, 1949).

The other national organization to which Marcus gave years of devoted and distinguished service was the Central Conference of American Rabbis. For many years he served as chairman of its Committee on Contemporary History and Literature. More importantly, he was elected to several terms on its Executive Board. Then, in 1949, his colleagues chose him to be president of the Conference.

He devoted himself unstintingly to the Conference during his two-year tenure as vice president, followed by his year as president. He gave it strong and forthright leadership, and he challenged his colleagues to make known their convictions, as he did, on current controversial issues. As president he never hesitated to champion an unpopular cause, if he felt it was just and right. This is seen most clearly in his presidential message, delivered in Cincinnati at the 61st annual convention of the Central Conference of American Rabbis. Of course not all of his recommendations to the Conference were controversial. Those who knew him well, knew that he was, and is, a deeply religious man. This is evidenced in his presidential message, in his words of praise for the Institute on Jewish Theology which he helped organize on the Cincinnati campus of the College, and which he recommended continuing the next year.

He was, however, bitterly opposed to any union of Church and State. In introducing his second recommendation to the Conference — the holding of an institute on Church and State — Marcus said:

> Your President sometimes suspects that all of us here, on earth, are too far removed from the true essence of God. This departure from religion is evidenced on the part of some sectarians in their attempt to harness the State to the chariot wheel of the churches. I am unalterably opposed to all this. One would think that men of this generation had read sufficient history to know that the legal union of Church and State for fourteen hundred years led to the violation of conscience and to the brutal, senseless slaughter of millions of human beings. The attempt to use the public school to further denominational religion is but one more phase of the attempt to use the power of the State to control conscience. . . . Any threat to the complete independence of the American public school system is a mortal threat to American democracy and ultimately to the equality of all religious minorities (*Central Conference of American Rabbis Yearbook [CCAR Yearbook]*, 60:238).

Marcus was a realist on four other religious issues to which he called attention in his presidential message. He believed that for both rabbis and lay persons, a "Guide" to Liberal Jewish Practice was essential to bring order out of chaos and to provide direction in matters of ritual, Sabbath, Holiday observances, and basic beliefs. In introducing his recommendation on developing a Guide to Liberal Jewish Practice, his wonderful sense of humor lightened the heaviness of the issue. He said that "one of my colleagues recently informed me that there is a host of young men who are in favor of the introduction of such a guide. In spite of the fact that they are for it, I still think that they are right." In a more serious vein, he went on to say:

> Gradually, over a period of years, your President has come to the conclusion that there is no conflict between idea and practice, between liberty and observance, always so long as there is no compulsion, expressed or implied. During the last 150 years, Liberal Judaism has built up its own *Torah she-be-al-peh*, its own unwritten law. It is time to set it down in black on white. We do stand for something (*CCAR Yearbook*, 60:239).

The second recommendation that Marcus proposed on religious matters called for a study as to how the rabbis could make the synagogue service more meaningful and more appealing, and how to make the total temple program more effective. He was deeply concerned with what he observed, in his travels throughout the country and his annual visits to scores of synagogues, to be the morass of congregational life.

Jewish education was a matter of deep concern for him. He felt that young people were leaving the synagogue in significant numbers because of boredom and lack of knowledge. Therefore, another recommendation that he presented to the Conference was for renewed emphasis on religious education, with particular focus on holding and deepening the commitment of our young people of confirmation and post-confirmation age.

Another recommendation on matters of religion was his vehement opposition to the merger of large congregations, creating "even greater behemoths." He called this practice "a crime against the spirit of our religion." He called for the creation of many small congregations and recommended that "this Conference go on record expressing its unqualified disapproval of any merger of congregations" (*CCAR Yearbook*, 60:243).

Finally, Marcus spoke out on the two matters that he considered of immediate importance: Jewish unity in America and our relationship to the State of Israel. For many years, in many different forums, he had urged the creation of a central body to speak on behalf of American Jewry. He now used the prestige of his office to recommend that "this Conference request the Council of Jewish Federations and Welfare Funds to call a meeting of all Jewish community councils for the purpose of creating a National American Jewish Assembly to the end that there will be one body that shall speak and act with authority for American Jewry" (p. 244). This vision has never been completely realized, but Marcus was one of the leaders who encouraged the creation of the National Jewish Community Relations Advisory Council. He approved its determination to concern itself with anti-Semitism and with positive community relations for American Jewry.

The most difficult of all the recommendations that President Marcus proposed to the Central Conference of American Rabbis were two regarding the State of Israel. He had always been a "lover of Zion," though never a registered political Zionist. Marcus' feelings about Israel are best expressed in the prelude to his tenth recommendation, regarding the situation of Reform rabbis in the State:

> Every Jew who has but a slight knowledge of the history of his people is conscious that we are living in millennial times. There has been no comparable age since the days of Judah Maccabee. . . . Today in the Third Commonwealth not thousands, but hundreds of thousands of Jews, from all over the world, from distant Afghanistan to the dark ghettos of Morocco, are pouring into the new land of Israel. It is a privilege to be alive in this age, to help write one of the most glorious pages of all Jewish history, and to witness this Messianic ingathering of the exiles. We love Israel and are zealous for its honor. The Israel that you and I treasure must not be just

another state characterized by an unmoral *raison d'état*, fighting and conniving for political advantage, living and falling by the standards that have created but also have also inevitably destroyed every great empire. If Israel is to remain only a city of refuge it may command our purses but not our veneration. If it is not to be Zion, then it will be but another duodecimo oriental principality doomed to fall at the first unfavorable conjunction of historic circumstances. If Israel is to begin its life in furtive expediency, with the denial of basic liberties to fellow Jews, what then can we hope for the future? Is this the prophetic dream? Today every obscure Moslem and Christian priest in Israel has complete equality as a religionist with all others. This is as it should be. Liberal Rabbis, with one exception, are not permitted to preside at marriages, at divorces, or to perform other functions which are denied no other group, Jewish or Gentile, in the land of Israel. . . . But we are asked not to disturb the delicate political balance in Israel. I have been counselled to remain silent. . . . If there is a single Jew in Israel who is deprived of his civil liberties because of his religion, then there is injustice in the Holy Land. There can be no compromise with wrong. We as Liberals, as rabbis, as Jews, as humanitarians, must protest, and I therefore recommend that this Conference denounce the injustice that now prevails in the land of Israel whereby some Reform rabbis are denied complete religious equality. We ask that Liberal Rabbis be granted the same rights as all other [i.e., Orthodox] rabbis, and equal rights with Christian and Moslem clergymen (*CCAR Yearbook*, 60:244-45)

Marcus concluded his presidential address urging that proper perspective be maintained in our relationship with the State of Israel and in our role in American Jewry. He summarized our obligations to both Israel and American Jewry in two remarkable paragraphs, ending with a passionate exhortation to his colleagues:

For obvious reasons Israel will occupy a disproportionate place in our spiritual economy. The greatest gift that we as communal religious and cultural leaders can bring to it is the unshakable determination to make that land worthy of itself. For us, as rabbis, this means spiritual, religious, and cultural aid. We must build its schools, its colleges and universities, and pour into that new republic the best that the world abroad has yet fashioned in science, in literature, in the arts, in the humanities. Built on the ruins of Turkish misgovernment and English colonial disdain, the land of our fathers has not yet attained the cultural *niveau* that distinguishes the western democracies. There are some who say that Zionism is dead, but I say unto you that there is a higher Zionism and that has only begun, and that is the task of again making Israel a Holy Land, a land of books and ideals, a land where new psalms will once more be written, a land to which all people will again stream that they may be reborn in that new faith that will yet glow on Judah's hills. Our task is to be sure that Israel never betrays herself and that once more she will rise again as Zion.

But this is only half our task. The other half is to make of American Jewry the greatest Jewish community the world has ever known. That is our mandate. I am not thinking in terms of numbers when I speak of greatness. I am speaking of greatness in terms of the spirit, of an America whose Jews read and study, who have a knowledge of their ancestral history, who are stirred with a sense of noblesse oblige. You may believe me when I tell you that in all the long story of our people, there was never a chosen generation such as this, there was never a Jewry as generous as this, as devoted, as self-respecting, as loyal and as honorable. You have never had finer clay than this yearning for the skillful hand of the potter. But we, the rabbis, must be fired with the consciousness of our opportunity, of the need to inform ourselves so that we may teach our people. If we can only enthrall them with the glory of being a Jew, then we shall be able to build a Jewish life on this soil that will produce philosophers, poets, and great human beings whose achievements will dwarf the writings and the very men in whom Poland, Spain, Babylon, Egypt, and Palestine once gloried. This is our hour for greatness. God grant us the moral courage and the spiritual strengh to respond to this, the greatest challenge ever presented to the Jewish leaders (*CCAR Yearbook*, 60:245-46).

Neither the political Zionists nor the anti-Zionists among the members of the Conference were pleased with the stand that Marcus took regarding the State of Israel and our relationship to it as American Jews. He was convinced that the future of twentieth-century Jewry depended on a strong, viable American Jewish community, and that included the survival of Israel, too. However, this attitude to Israel was similar to that of Asher Ginsberg's cultural Zionists. He was wary of the political complexities of the rival parties in Israel, and of their willingness to compromise on ethical issues for the sake of power. In this stance, Marcus alienated many Zionists. But the anti-Zionists were never satisfied either with his support for the principles of Zion. In facing both extremes and maintaining firmly that American Jewry must retain leadership both here and abroad in effectively pursuing its own messianic hopes, Marcus demonstrated his conviction and his courage as one of the great rabbinic leaders of Jewry.

Dr. Marcus' next major address to colleagues and future colleagues was the Ordination Sermon for the Hebrew Union College Class of 1974 in Cincinnati. He was genuinely touched by the fact that the Class itself had chosen him to be their ordination speaker. Marcus had never retired from the Faculty, though his teaching load had decreased to one course or seminar each semester. In addition there were a number of students who wrote theses and dissertations under him. Of course, most of the students did not get to know him as well as students of bygone years, when he had taught fifteen or more hours each semester and was deeply involved in all aspects of the College life. Still, there were each year a few "chosen ones" who were privileged to know "the Doctor" well and to work for him on a variety of projects. Most important, though, the Marcus tradition and spirit were alive and respected on the campus. Most from afar, and a few more intimately, felt a deep affection for this living legend in American Jewish life. Choosing Professor Marcus to speak at their ordination was the way the class of '74 chose to express that affection.

Though almost eighty years old, Marcus rose to the occasion. He delivered a magnificent sermon, "The Larger Task." Of course, he reminded the congregation of a favorite Marcus adage: "The sun never sets on a graduate of the Hebrew Union College." Then, in his closing exhortation, he challenged the class:

> Consider yourselves men of destiny. You are our future. The eternity of our people and our faith is bound up in your soul. You must be the incarnation of Jewish learning and morality, carrying with you, wherever you go, our exalted tradition, our spiritual homeland which is as wide as the world itself, as high as the heavens, and as comforting as a mother's love. Thirty centuries of Hebraic, Israelite, and Judaic idealism and learning are challenging you to go forward. Never succumb to doubt; constantly affirm that the Jew and Judaism will abide. We have already survived a dozen holocausts, bearing witness to the world that a people lives by the quality of its loyalties. The weapons that have saved us are not chariots, not horses, not tanks, not missiles, but our books, our learning, our Torah.
>
> And what, I pray you, is Torah, in its ultimate essence, but love, justice, peace, compassion, tolerance, the relentless determination to save ourselves and our fellow-man through the creation of a new universal moral society. That is our only salvation.

So now we turn to you, the generation in whom lies our hope for a better world. "Ride on and prosper." And may the God of our fathers give you the courage, so to rise to ever greater spiritual and intellectual heights, that you and all of us may cry out, triumphantly and exultantly, to all the ages yet to come: "I shall not die but live, and declare the works of the Lord." And so may it be.

The professor was ever the optimist. And this optimism was more than just wishful thinking or Pollyanna-like cheer. His optimism stemmed from a deep conviction, born of our Jewish tradition, that human beings are innately good, and that we have the potential to serve as partners with God in establishing God's Kingdom on earth. This faith in the future was expressed exquisitely in *Testament: A Personal Statement*, an address which he delivered in Cincinnati in June, 1989, at the Sabbath morning service of the Centennial Assembly of the Central Conference of American Rabbis. He considered this his valedictory, though his colleagues look forward to more glorious moments of inspiration and learning with him in the years to come.

In this memorable centennial address, Dr. Marcus expressed his confidence in the future for the Jew in America and to American Jewry's capacity for leadership in undergirding the future of Israel and of Diaspora Jewry. "This is truly a golden age," he said. "How fortunate you are to be alive in this the most glorious moment in all Jewish history." Then, with a twinkle in his eye, and with that characteristic gentle humor for which he has always been so well known, he quoted the prophet, Jeremiah (31:16) "*Ronu le-yaakov simhoh*, sing with gladness for Jacob" (*Testament*, p. 2).

Marcus did have a solemn warning, though, for those assembled:

. . . we face a serious problem — not oppression to be sure — but constant attrition, assimilation. Yes, we are assimilating, declining numerically. Don't draw any false conclusions. Do not misread Jewish history. In the three-to-four thousand years there was never a day when the majority of Jews were practicing religionists, not even in ancient Israel in the ninth century before the Christian era. The majority of all Jews in Palestine were then virtual pagans. In the days of Elijah there were only 7,000 practicing Jews in all of Israel, men and women who had not bowed the knee to Baal. Today we are few not because we were murdered throughout the ages but because we seceded, acculturated, voluntarily. I surmise that most Jews in history assimilated, succumbed to the attractive appeal of the host culture. Otherwise we would not be a mere 13,000,000 but 1,000,000,000, as numerous as the Chinese. In all the centuries the handful who survived was the norm. Jochanan ben Zakkai was no fool; when he defected to the Romans all he asked for was a little schoolhouse and a few disciples. Forget about numbers. Numbers are a myth. We have always lived through a few, a saving remnant.

Jewish history points to a statistical moral. If we are determined to survive — and we are — we must cultivate those few who are devoted to our religion, our culture. When you survey your congregation on a Friday night, don't count bodies, count souls.

Those chosen few, this elect, has a job to do: these Jews are our future; they have to save us; even more they have something to tell the whole world, to distill for all humanity what the Jew has learned after 3,000 years of bitter experience. We are presumptuous enough to bring our gifts to the Gentiles, to those who, we believe, are desperately in need of what we have to offer. We do not wish to missionize the nations; we want to humanize them. And what is this that we have learned; what are the implacable, but the inexorable verities? It is our hope to further traditional values, not traditions as such. We must become proud exponents of the best in our Jewish heritage. That legacy reached its height in the ethical demands of the Hebrew prophets. They taught us to abhor hatred, violence, brutality, to avoid every aspect of any concept that manifests itself in contempt for fellow human beings. . . . Our ultimate goal is to strive for a universal society which will require political states to maintain the same ethical standards that distinguish moral individuals. We Jews pride ourselves that we are a civilized humanitarian folk. Let us manifest it in all of our actions. Our history demands that we continue our quest for Zion. Zion is our highest Jewish self in projection; it is the ideal we seek but we can only glimpse.

Rabbi Marcus, *divine nehomoh*? Comfort? The true *nehomoh* is to face reality. We address ourselves to eternity. We have an enduring faith. We have no choice; for this were we created. The bodies consumed in Auschwitz may yet light up a world that lives in darkness. "Our ancestors received the law on Sinai's mount amidst thunder and lightning and cloud and flame, and amidst thunder and lightning and cloud and flame we will keep it." Our prophetic exhortations are the last and best hope of humanity. If we raise but a handful of disciples who treasure our ideals, we will survive. We are an *am olom*, an eternal people; the world can never, never destroy all of us. And in that fateful moment when the earth begins to shatter, when the very heavens tremble, when the sun, the moon and the stars turn dark, when the last bomb falls and the last mushroom cloud evaporates, we, we will emerge erect, undaunted, dedicated to the hope that a day will yet come when "they shall not hurt nor destroy in all my Holy Mountain, for the earth shall be full of the knowledge of the Lord as the waters cover the sea" (Isa. 11:9) (*Testament*, pp. 4-6).

The standing ovation that followed Marcus' address was prolonged and heartfelt. Every man and woman crowded into the Plum Street Temple felt that they were standing in the presence of greatness. Jacob Rader Marcus was a teacher and colleague for whom they had profound admiration and genuine affection. He had become a symbol of all that was noblest and most respected in the American Jewish community.

12. IN APPRECIATION

Marcus has even disproved the ancient adage that no man was ever a prophet in his own community. The city of Cincinnati, in which he has lived his entire adult life, knows and loves him, too. In the 1930's, when Hitler spewed his virulent anti-Semitism throughout Europe, and fascist organizations echoed his views in the heartland of America, Jacob Marcus was the one Jew in Cincinnati who went from church to church attacking the Nazi philosophy. He was highly respected in the Christian community, and though Cincinnatians were certainly not anti-German, they listened to him, and they applauded his courageous stand against anti-Semitism. A decade later, he became chairman of the Cincinnati Jewish Community Relations Committee. One of the major concerns of the committee, during his tenure as chairman, was the fact that one of the largest industries in the city had a policy of hiring no Jews. Because of Marcus' prestige and persistence, this issue was confronted by both Jewish and Christian groups, as well as by civic organizations. Ultimately this great corporation changed its policy. As a result, today the pattern of non-discrimination is the norm in Cincinnati.

The Cincinnati community showered its kudos on this man in many ways. The academic community was first. Marcus was given honorary doctorates by both Xavier University, Cincinnati's Jesuit institution, and by the University of Cincinnati. These are but two of the seven honorary degrees that have been conferred upon him, but two that he prizes highly.

Five years ago, on the occasion of the fiftieth anniversary

of his residency at 401 McAlpin Avenue, the duplex he purchased shortly after his marriage, and the only home in which he and his family have resided, the city of Cincinnati honored him by naming the corner on which he lives Marcus Square. Shortly thereafter, the Cincinnati Club, the most prestigious private club in the city gave him its annual award as an outstanding citizen of the community. This was followed by Marcus' becoming the recipient of the very important Post-Corbett Award, the most highly coveted civic recognition in Cincinnati. Later a consortium of colleges and universities in the Cincinnati area bestowed on Dr. Marcus its award as the outstanding teacher of the year.

When asked which of the honors he has received over the years means the most to him, Dr. Marcus is quick to respond: becoming the Honorary President of the Central Conference of American Rabbis. This is the highest recognition that colleagues and former students can bestow, and when all is said and done, he is first and foremost a rabbi. And he takes his responsibility to prepare students for the rabbinate very seriously. For many years, he has addressed the freshman class at the College in Cincinnati on the practical aspects of the rabbinate. He discusses their personal code of conduct and their relationships with junior and senior colleagues, with their Board of Trustees, and with their congregations. He becomes very specific in listing what he calls the Marcusian laws of the rabbinate, and he concludes by listing the positive aspects of this profession which make it the noblest of all vocations. The sound advice contained in this talk has also been repeated to the senior classes over the years.

Men and women, representing several generations have listened intently to Marcus' practical wisdom and have taken it to heart. That is why his telephone has continued to ring almost daily through the years with rabbis of all ages seeking his advice on the issues and the personal problems with which they must cope. This is also the reason that at the annual meetings of the Central Conference of American Rabbis, which Marcus has attended regularly, his little black book is filled with appointments with colleagues who seek his counsel. No matter how weary he becomes, he never turns down a request for an appointment. And when he does take time to visit on the convention floor, he is besieged by men and women who just want to shake his hand and manifest their affection.

These same men and women continue to seek their mentor as a speaker for special occasions in their congregations. Only in recent years has he begun a drastic curtailment of his speaking engagements. Now he accepts only one or two invitations a year, just to prove to himself that at 98 he still has the ability to hold an audience and to perform well enough to give himself a grade of 90.

His lifestyle has always been a simple one. His home is comfortable, though by no means ostentatious., Until the past few years he enjoyed a drink with friends before a meal. And he thoroughly enjoys good food: fresh fish, Chinese cuisine and, of course, all the traditional Jewish dishes. He never over-indulges, though, and he watches his weight very carefully. He rarely engages in recreational activities beyond occasional dinners and social evenings with friends. In bygone times, when he was completely drained by his heavy work schedule, he would close his books and in the middle of the afternoon go downtown with a friend or a student to enjoy a real movie binge. They would see two or three westerns or detective mysteries, pausing only for a bit of supper. He would then return home, tired but refreshed. Though his movie-going days are over, he still reads a mystery or western novel each night before retiring.

Each one of us—Marcus' student secretaries, assistants in the early years of the Archives, his seminar scholars, and those who wrote theses and dissertations under him—each one enjoyed a special relationship with "the Doctor." As an eighteen-year-old college sophomore from the Deep South,

I arrived at the Hebrew Union College totally unprepared for this bewildering world of Jews and Jewish scholarship. Fortunately my own rabbi, Ira Sanders, was a close personal friend of Marcus. Through the introduction he provided, I was fortunate to meet the Doctor my first week on the campus. He evidently saw at once that I was as much a greenhorn there as were those who arrived on the latest boat from Europe, so he made himself available as a friend and counsellor, and he guided me through those first baffling weeks of adjustment to a way of life that was so foreign to me. Dozens of times in those first months I was ready to pack my bag and return to my home. It was Marcus and the comfort and security of his study that kept me on the right path. Then he made me his secretary, though my typing was poor and my shorthand nonexistent. Through these next years he became my role model. He is my idea of what a scholar and teacher should always be. He is a man of unquestionable integrity, a gentleman in every relationship, and a wise student of human nature. He is a good listener and a trusted confidant. In the darkest hours following the loss of my sister and my father, he was there for me, quietly compassionate. When crucial decisions faced me as the years went by, he was an understanding guide through the complexities of career choices and congregational expectations. How a man with such heavy faculty responsibilities, with such high goals in his field of scholarship, with such a demanding schedule of lectures throughout the country, and with his own difficult family burdens, how such a man could find time not only for meeting my needs, but those of scores of students like me, in Cincinnati and throughout the rabbinate, I'll never know. His work day was, and continues to be, at least sixteen hours a day, six days a week. But—let me repeat—he has never been known to refuse to make an appointment with a student, or to refuse to answer long distance calls from former students in far-flung congregations. And this is true to this day! He is the rabbi's rabbi, in every sense of the word.

142

Many of his "chasidim" have sought to summarize the character, the personality, the scholarly erudition, the platform charisma that is Jacob Rader Marcus. His student and close friend, the late Bertram Korn, captured the essence of the man best in one paragraph that he wrote in his preface to *A Bicentennial Festschrift for Jacob R. Marcus*, published in 1976:

> Marcus is a unique figure in the Reform rabbinate, in American Jewish scholarly circles, and in the Cincinnati Jewish community. There simply is no one like him: a human being who evokes love and appreciation; a scholar who sacrifices no single element of his demanding standards while seeing something of value in even the least scientific piece of work; a teacher who conveys a sense of the drama and tragedy and mystery and zest of history; an American who loves this country and believes in its destiny; a Jew who is committed to the One Lord and loves everything about His people's life and experience, the greatness as well as the pain and pathos; a Reform Jew who still maintains the conviction that a liberal interpretation of his historic heritage will help Western civilization as well as the Jews to survive the dangers of the coming era. May God give him and us many years of his kindness and wisdom, his friendship and learning (p. xi).

And may we, his students and his disciples, ever seek to keep foremost in our minds Jacob Marcus' highest moral imperative: "The most important thing in life is integrity."